CONTENTS

Printed in the United States of America

First Printing, 2019

Paperback: ISBN 9781792147395

www.DavidOnEarth.com

To the one for whom I would abandon all things here on earth.

Without you the next page would be blank.

INTRODUCTION

I was approached by several friends to write about my experience hiking the Colorado Trail (CT) in 2018. Initially I resisted the idea. When compared to other great human feats, it didn't seem to rank very high in the amazing achievements category. It's a nice trail to write about; it's beautiful. But the CT is not the longest or most difficult trail in the world or even in America. I didn't break any records. I don't have a dramatic survival story. On the surface this was merely a (slightly more than) middle-aged guy hiking 500 miles through Colorado. Granted, that might sound like an enormous feat to some people, but it's not terribly uncommon. Did I even have a story? Would my story be compelling enough? Would anyone be interested?

As I explored these questions it occurred to me that perhaps I did have something to tell. What I came to realize is that it was *my* story. We all have a story. It's our own; it's no one else's. It's unique as we are. And if I am worthy enough to be, to exist, my story is worth telling simply because it is mine.

Another factor that influenced this telling is that I like to encourage people to step out of their day-to-day lives and do the thing they love to do. Take a risk. Be purposeful. Dare to be happy. Set yourself up to smile and enjoy every breath. Whatever it is, find a way to make it happen. Travel the world, grow a vegetable garden, open a business, run a marathon, start a nonprofit, paint a picture, learn how to play piano, spend more time with the kids... do whatever fulfills you and makes you happy or gives you a passion for living.

To live is such an amazing gift. It's a gift that invites us to experience it in full. We shouldn't squander what we have on things that are less than amazing.

I also had a strong sense of purpose that carried me through those 41 days on the CT. It was all quite intentional. It was irresistibly compelling. And I like those kinds of stories regardless of the ending. I suspect other people do as well.

Although I am not in the class of superstar adventurers who have earned far greater credentials, there are years of lessons I've learned that may help someone who is considering a great adventure such as the CT. These things are worth telling.

So, for all those reasons I gave myself to the pursuit of this writing.

I heard the clock ticking. It started years ago. At the age of 16 I was diagnosed with a heart condition, a faulty valve, that in 34 years would demand a corrective procedure. Then in 2004 I had an open-heart surgery that would provisionally set the stage for my activities in 2018.

They placed a prosthetic ring in my heart to keep my mitral valve functioning properly. My wife of 36 years, Bobbi, likes to call it "my precious" (think: Lord of the Rings). My Precious had a life cycle that would start deteriorating after 15 years of use. At least, this is what I was told when they put it in me. I discovered recently that lifespan estimates for these rings have proven to be significantly longer. Regardless of when, another corrective surgery would follow at some point during the ring's inevitable degradation.

Because I don't like to live with regrets and I knew my days for physically demanding activities would someday be limited beyond my control, 2018 was the year for me to get it done, the year before My Precious would turn 15. The "it" turned out to be hiking the CT. I wasn't so sure about when my next corrective surgery would be or what my prognosis would be afterward. But I knew one thing: I was not going to wait for it to make my decisions for me. "This is my time", I thought. It's now or it may be never. Tick, tock.

Over the past few years Bobbi worked with me so we could pay off our mortgage. We worked our way to very little debt and a retirement plan that was well on the way to maturity.

Despite being in a relatively good physical and financial position for me to hike the CT, she expressed some reservation. But she was also wise enough to understand and has borne witness to the fact that we all ultimately have little control over our futures. She knew that holding me back from what I thought was important for me might cause her regret should I never have the chance to do this again. For whatever reason, her protest was light. Her blessing was given. I now had all I needed to be fully empowered to pursue this adventure, possibly the greatest outdoor adventure of my lifetime.

Bobbi has learned to tolerate my adventurous spirit and has come to trust that I take all the necessary precautions to be safe while I'm out in the wild. I had hiked over 30 of the 14,000-foot peaks in Colorado and spent many days hiking and a good amount of time backpacking. She knew that I would do everything I could to make this CT experience a safe and cautioned trek.

Now I had to figure out the job situation. I wasn't in such a desperate position that I couldn't take some time off of work to do something like this. And the job market was favorable if I couldn't work something out with my current employer. So, a few weeks before I started the trail I had resigned my position as a senior IT manager at a leading satellite technology company. When I announced my move to people at work I had nothing but positive responses, some may even have been a little envious. This felt affirming. When I mentioned my job resignation while I was on the trail, most people applauded the gutsy move. But from my perspective I wasn't taking a big unemployment risk. It wasn't about a hatred for the job. I wasn't "sticking it to the man". True, after nearly 40 years of working, I felt it was time for a break. It wasn't a mean-spirited departure. I simply felt like this was the time for me to do this. I had been loosely planning over the past couple years and more intently in the months leading up to the hike. My employer was given many months advanced notice. I was physically, mentally, and financially ready to make this move. So, I did, because it was my time.

In the pages to follow I have written about what prepared me for this hike. I have also summarized my time on the trail and some thoughts after the hike. There are 31 "pro tips" throughout the reading that offer some practical advice and ideas for making life better on the trail. In the final chapters I've included my gear list and some common questions and answers.

I hope readers are encouraged by my purpose for this adventure and how that purpose evolved and became more tangible and powerful as the hike progressed.

I know one thing: this 500-mile hike I took into the Colorado wilderness that has been GREAT for me. It doesn't need to be great for anyone else. As it's been said: You be you and I'll be me. But whoever you are, do your thing with purpose and with extraordinary prejudice.

Lastly, I want to thank the staff and volunteers at the Colorado Trail Foundation. This journey would not have been possible without their relentless love and support for this trail and the people who travel its path. They played a large part of my preparation before I began, my safety as I hiked, and have given me a platform to help others do the same. A portion of all sales of this book in whatever format will be donated to them as a small expression of my appreciation for what they have done for me.

Happy reading! Happy trails!
David on Earth

CHAPTER ONE

The Way Back

Adventures are often viewed as a way forward, a breaking into new territory, a doorway to discovery and freedom. Adventures can also be a way of finding missing pieces to the large puzzle of our lives. Adventures can help complete the natural continuity of life and spirit between our past, present, and future. My hike of the CT was about all these things. It became profoundly relevant.

I grew up in the Upper Peninsula of Michigan (U.P.). Just to be clear, the U.P. is not the northern part of the "glove". It's the often-forgotten piece of Michigan, north and west of the glove separated by the Mackinaw Bridge from the Lower Peninsula of Michigan (the glove). It shares its southern border with Wisconsin and northern border with Lake Superior. I've always been surprised when I meet people who don't realize there is more to Michigan than the glove.

Much of this land is forested and very sparsely populated. It contains only about 3% of Michigan's total population yet makes up nearly 30% of Michigan's landmass. (Bureau) If you are from the U.P. you're a "Yooper" (pronounce: you-per). If "Holy-Wah! Didjoo see da size adat moose?" sounds normal, you're probably a Yooper. Feel the pride.

With all this wilderness and so few people, it's no wonder

that outdoor activities fill the lives of Yoopers. Hunting, fishing, ice fishing, trapping, camping, skiing, snowshoeing, hiking – it's part of how people exist in the U.P. I was no exception to embracing this identity. Watching the northern lights (aurora borealis) in the fall, looking for agates and sand worn colored glass on the shores of Lake Superior, hiking the Porkies and the Norwich Bluff, exploring the forests around our house, snowmobiling to our camp near Fourteen Mile Point, and on and on. Such was the life of this young Yooper.

This love I have of the outdoors didn't start with me or my generation. Its history is long and colored. Before the days of my parents and their parents... and their parents, my 5th great grandfather, Dominick Brunette Sr., had been among the first fur traders to settle in the Green Bay, Wisconsin area in 1798 at the age of 19. The young fearless French explorer has been written about in several printings at the Wisconsin Historical Society. (Identities 2018) As has my 7th great grandfather, Charles Michel De Langlade, who is known as the Father of Wisconsin. His "relationship to the Ottawa and his great prestige as a soldier were valuable assets when he and his father established a trading post at Green Bay around 1745". (Society 2018) No doubt the exploits, toughness, and the love and respect for the wild has been passed down through the generations.

In my youth I made my way through the ranks of the Cub Scouts and then Boy Scouts. I didn't quite achieve Eagle Scout, but I came close – still worth mentioning. Camping, hiking, and every merit badge that had to do with being active in the outdoors was proudly hand-sewn by me on my sash. Badge presentation ceremonies were not to be missed; they were applauded and celebrated with as much honor and tradition as a young teen could demonstrate.

One backpacking trip I took with Boy Scout Troop 209 was to Isle Royale. A 6-day adventure – my longest up to my CT attempt – along the Green Stone Ridge on the remote preserve island crowned a National Park in the northern part of Lake Superior. It's 45 miles long and 9 miles wide within an area of 207 square miles, yet without a single permanent resident. (N. P. Service 2018) It's a naturalist's paradise. A person travels to this place by ferry from ports on the Keweenaw Peninsula in Upper Michigan or in northeastern Minnesota. Being dropped on a remote island to fend for ourselves for the week was exciting. We were exploring a new place, exercising all our scouting skills, and proving to ourselves and to others that we had what it took to do this. Of course, we had adult chaperones who probably did more for us than we realized, but we all approached this adventure with great personal responsibility.

The details have mostly taken a deep dive in the dark recesses of my memory, but I would venture to guess it was a 30-mile trip. The part I still vividly recall is the freedom of the trail and the unblemished wildness of the experience. We climbed up a fire tower to see the entire island. We gorged on thumb-size wild blueberries on a hillside. We had a close encounter with a cow moose and her calf. We navigated with maps and compasses as we made our way up, over, and through the core of the island. Our gear included external framed packs, aluminum cook sets, flannel lined sleeping bags, and canvas pup tents. We heated water for our freeze-dried meals over an open fire. We boiled our drinking water and used purification tablets – no filters. We dipped our wooden matches in wax to waterproof them. We had heavy leather boots, the bigger the better. There was no such thing as ultralight gear. We didn't do selfies or take pictures of our food. Our eyes and minds were fixed on the wonderfully wild world around us.

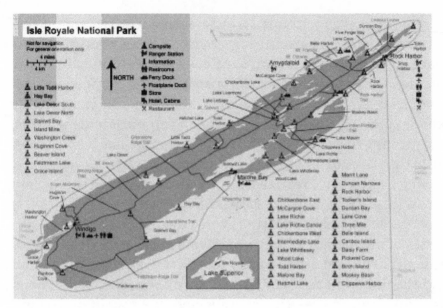

Figure 1 - Isle Royale

Time sure has changed our gear and some of our habits. Today, ultralight is the hype and everything else is not. But what time has not changed for me is the value of the experience and the reasons I'm attracted to the wilderness.

The continuity of life and spirit for me is the freedom, sense of adventure, and the completeness I feel when my feet are on a trail in a wild place. When I'm surrounded by the purity of nature, I feel that I am an integrated part this world. It feels like home. It feels right. It feels like I've been transported in a small way back to the days of my French fir trading ancestors as they settled the Green Bay Wisconsin area. It's my way back. It's how I am best in the present. And it's how I can see forward. I can say with a good amount of certainty that it's where I find my identity and my purpose.

CHAPTER TWO

Can I do This?

A couple years before my CT attempt, I was busy peak bagging. I was trying to climb as many 14,000-foot peaks (14ers) in Colorado as I could fit into my schedule. Several of those climbs were 15 or more miles long. One of my hiking partners, Brian, mentioned the challenge of the CT and asked of himself and me if we could do such a long day consecutively for weeks on end. At the time it seemed quite overwhelming both physically and mentally.

It's Eventually More Mental

Most people who have experience with long hikes will say that the trail quickly becomes a mental challenge more than a physical challenge. That's not to say that it becomes easy or that there won't be injuries due to fatigue. During the first part of the trail the mental state probably has much to do with the physical struggle. But soon, as the body toughens, the mental challenge becomes the greater and different kind of struggle as the immensity and toughness of the task is realized. This may be because physical challenges are tangible. They can more easily be defined and can programmatically be addressed with the right physical conditioning or medical attention.

The mental part is not so tangible. It's harder to train and few people have a systematic way of conditioning the mind to overcome the trail's challenges. How will a person handle being away from home, being alone for long periods of time, being out of cell service, living without modern luxuries, hiking in the rain and cold, constantly fighting the elements, eating the same boring food every day, and being dirty and stinky all the time?

Everyone is different, of course. What mentally wears on one person might not on another. The simplest and seemingly easiest thing to overcome for one might be completely overwhelming for another. The mental challenge is a complex challenge.

I always believed myself to be one who could be physically trained for just about any endurance test. And I consider myself to be tenacious beyond reason at times, given that I care enough about the result. So, when I asked myself if I could do this, my thinking was: "Yes, I probably can". But, that's easy to say and I would know for sure soon enough.

It's not a Day Hike

One in five who start the Appalachian Trail with the intention of finishing will drop out within the first few days. Why? It's not because they are injured. I suspect it may be because of misguided expectations. They thought it was going to be like a long day hike or backpacking trip. Thru-hiking is not a day hike and it's not a backpacking trip.

Thru-hiking requires:
- much lighter weight gear considerations, whereas day hikers have much less concern over the weight of their gear
- more calorie dense foods, whereas a day hiker can bring gourmet meals with a full camping cook set
- more physical and mental preparation, whereas day hikers can go without much or any prep work
- financial planning, whereas day hikers have no financial planning to consider
- greater long-term disciplines, whereas day

hikers only need to survive the day (or a few days if backpacking the weekend)

It's usually no big deal if a person forgets an item of gear or doesn't take enough snacks on a day hike. In a few hours the problem will be solved. Not true for a thru-hiker. Forgetting a piece of gear or having a gear item break down could make the hike very uncomfortable. Not bringing enough food could mean that there will be days without eating much in an environment where 4000 calories or more are burned every day.

Light weight gear is not a primary consideration for day hikers. For thru-hikers every ounce is challenged. A person going on a few-day backpacking trip will hike 5-10 miles per day carrying a 50-pound pack. For most thru-hikers a 30-pound pack fully loaded with 5 days of food and a couple liters of water is probably close to the heaviest pack they will ever carry on the hike. And they will hike between 10 and 30 miles per day. This isn't to say that packs can't be heavier and miles can't be less, but most people who attempt a thru-hike are lighter with longer distances per day.

On a day hike a person can blast through a bunch of miles one day and rest the next day. A thru-hiker needs to think strategically. Resting the next day is usually not realistic. Pushing too hard often causes injury.

Referring to what Brian asked earlier: could I do a long day hike for weeks on end? The answer is: no, but I might be able to thru-hike if I take some time to figure out how this is different from my normal day hikes.

<u>Get the Financing Right</u>

Figuring how to stay financially afloat while away on a thru-hike is a necessary chore. Financial obligations need to be satisfied. Some people will eliminate as much financial obligation as possible before starting – paying off the house or getting out of a lease agreement; canceling TV and garbage pickup services. Other people will choose to pay bills in advance or arrange to have someone pay the bills on time. This requires time and planning so that money can be set aside to handle these things.

If the person is not retired, it also helps to have an employment plan in place for after the trail. I had several options for getting back to work. One of them worked out.

Build a Strong Support System

It takes a very strong person to do something big without supporters. A good piece of advice is to tell everyone when the decision has been made to do a thru-hike. Get people excited. Get people to help you. Find people to cheer you on. It then becomes a "we" thing and not a "me" thing. People are genuinely motivated to become part of something bigger than they are. When you succeed, they succeed too because they are an invested partner. And then when on-trail, contact this support system to let them know how it's going and ask again for support as needed. Know that it's very tough to go this alone. Build a support system.

My family had to be my biggest support; without their approval and willingness to help I probably would not have done this. I also had friends cheering me on and who helped with resupplies during the adventure. Many people played a role in making this achievable.

An Alternative

If for whatever reason you feel you are not ready to do the entire thru-hike but you still want to experience the trail, there is an alternative: section hiking. Hike sections of the trail each year, finishing in several years. This reduces the stressors that come with doing the whole trail at once, but in some respects, it may be tougher because it's like starting over every year. I hiked the final section of the CT with a guy named Ron who took seven years to hike the CT. It was no less of an achievement and celebration for Ron as it was for me.

Answer the Why – The Key to It All

There was still one thing that was missing from my planning, maybe the most important element. I needed a solid reason. I needed a strong purpose that would compel me to finish this trail, to help me overcome the challenges that would threaten my will to carry on.

Liz Thomas is among the most celebrated hikers in the U.S. with over 15,000 miles and 16 long distance hikes to her credit. Within the first few pages of her book *Long Trails* she writes about the importance of finding the "why" and that this might be the most important element of succeeding at any long-distance hike. (Thomas 2017)

I took her advice – it's hard to improve upon - and developed my "why". And I am so glad I did. I had to remind myself about my why several times during my hike. Without it, I may not have been strong enough to finish the trail.

Guided by Liz, I considered why I wanted to do this journey now, the rewards I was expecting, what I would be sacrificing, what apprehensions did I have, and what might help me succeed or fail at this adventure.

This exercise seemed a bit academic at first. But then as I stepped back to put it all in perspective with the bigger picture. I thought about where I came from. I considered how spending time in the wilderness somehow completes me. It all started to come into focus.

This was a great exercise. I realized that this isn't just a thing I wanted to do this summer. It became clear to me that I am supposed to do this hike. Not to sound too dramatic, but it was almost like I was fulfilling a destiny. It was becoming not a question of *if* I *can* do this but a question of *when* I *will* do this.

CHAPTER THREE

The Preparation

How does a person prepare for a 500-mile walk through the mountains of Colorado? The true answer is that there is no amount of preparation that can be done to make this easy or without challenges. However, this doesn't relieve a person from being prepared. I would not advise putting some stuff in your backpack in the morning and beginning a thru-hike in the afternoon. On the other hand, I've known people who were totally obsessed with being ready that they overtrained and injured themselves before starting. Obviously, the best preparation is somewhere between do-nothing and do-too-much. That's some copout advice, so let's get into the details.

Physical Prep

One prominent question among those wanting to prepare for a thru-hike is "what kind of physical training should I do before the hike?" This is a question that will have a specific answer for everyone because we are all in a different state of physical preparedness.

There are many long-distance hikers who will say they do no (or little) physical conditioning before their hikes. These people are typically not overweight, young, and in good physical condition already. In which case I'd say, "You'll be fine."

For the rest of us who are either overweight, older, out of shape, or maybe all those things - the best advice is to put some focused effort toward becoming physically prepared.

No matter what age or condition a person is in, being physically ready is never bad advice. Some people just have more work to do than others. But know one thing: no matter how much training a person does, the trail will be the real trainer.

The trail is a unique beast that can't be effectively replicated in a gym. The gym is good for strength training and learning stretching techniques. The trail is good for environmental conditioning. What do I mean by this?

The goals here are to 1) complete the trail without injury and 2) make the transition to full-time hiking as painless as possible. Using both the gym and the trail is a good balanced approach.

- The gym is a great place to strengthen and condition primary muscle groups.
- The trail teaches a person so many other things, like: how to move for long periods of time with extra weight on the back, how to manage rest periods, and how to react to changes in the environment.

Get in the Gym

I'm not a physical trainer. So, first thing I would advise is to consult with a trainer who can create a training program to meet your goals, which may involve some customization for your unique needs. For instance, I've known hikers who have chronic ankle problems. Those people could benefit from a program that helps address strengthening the ankles.

From my experience I would expect the trainer to focus on core training (making your midsection strong), endurance training (strengthening your cardiovascular strength system to better endure the stress, pain, and fatigue of the trail). I would also expect some attention to leg strength and lessons on stretching exercises to do before, during, and after each day's hike.

Get on the Trail

The second component of physical training is spending time on the trail. Your body needs to know how to cope with and react to trail conditions. Time on trails that are similar to the CT will further strengthen various muscle groups because you will be going through the actual movements. It will also help you develop your pace and cadence for different ascending and descending conditions. The trail will also teach you how to lessen the impact on your frame through different techniques such as speed adjustments, feet placement, body positioning, posture, and muscle controls.

I also suggest that when a person trains on the trail that they carry their backpack and slowly increase the pack weight to full pack weight near the end of the training program. This will help your body adjust to the additional weight.

The ratio of gym to trail time should be at least 1 to 2, in my opinion. For every hour spent in the gym a person should spend at least two hours on the trail. Others may suggest a different ratio, but because the trail has taught me nearly everything I need to do and has kept me from injury, I put more emphasis there.

When should a person start training? For people that are mostly inactive, I would suggest 120 days from start date. This time can be reduced for those who are more active.

Additionally, a couple of techniques that have helped me sustain good trail speed without causing fatigue on climbs are the "Rest Step for Uphill" and "Avoiding Downhill Knee Pain".

Rest Step for Uphill

One technique I learned on the trail is the Rest Step. This is a technique used while ascending. It works like this: pause motion in the rear leg with it vertical and fully extended while the front leg takes the step (and full weight), pushing the body up. (Doran 2018) Several illustrations of this can be found on the Internet. The idea here is that one leg gets a brief rest with every step, reducing fatigue and stress. I showed one hiker this technique. He was able to get up hills with fewer breaks and less cardiovascular stress – he was breathing easier.

Avoid Downhill Knee Pain

There are also techniques for going downhill that can reduce knee and muscle pain. This technique includes these tips: relax, take shorter steps, don't lean back, lean slightly forward, keep knees slightly bent, use trekking poles for stabilization, go a little faster, and alternately shift the impact from knees and primary leg muscles to hips. (Bumgardner 2018)

Mental Prep

It would be easy to believe that mental toughness can't be trained, that it's either part of who you are or it's not. But modern science proves this to be an oversimplification and that mental toughness can, in fact, be learned. (Brown 2017)

Some studies suggest that being mindful is the answer to building strong mental stamina. Without getting into too much detail, a person can be taught to balance emotions, extinguish fear, pause to consider options before acting, build on conviction and morality, and become more intuitive. (Rathbun 2016) People who become mentally tough have confidence in themselves, they embrace challenges, they have a strong sense of control over their lives, and they are committed to achieving outcomes. (Mariama 2015) These are attributes that will benefit a person tremendously while on a long hike. If these are not already well developed and are not included as part of the hike preparation, the thru-hike may prove to be more challenging.

It seems logical that if mental toughness can be learned, it should be practiced and exercised as part of any "work out" routine before and during the hike. The solution: simply, hike a lot. Go out every day that you can. Take hikes that are long and hard. Takes hikes that have a steep incline and decline. Take hikes that are challenging both technically and mentally. Hike in the rain and in the cold. Be uncomfortable for long periods, days even. Just get out there and learn what it takes to handle the mental challenges of the trail. There's nothing like actually doing something to help us learn how to do it.

Another method of mentally preparing is to study the trail. Learn what you are about to do. If it's going to be a tough day, know that ahead of time, set expectations, envision yourself doing it, calculate the effort, and fully accept the challenge.

The trail will teach you what you need to know. Embrace all that it offers, all the ups and all the downs. It will make you mentally stronger.

Financial Prep

Being on the trail obviously means not being at work earning income. A person needs to take care of financial obligations before hitting the trail. This isn't just for the sake of staying out of financial trouble. It's also about having peace of mind while on the trail. No one needs financial worries while trying to enjoy the peace and freedom of the wilderness.

Before leaving for my CT hike I was told that a person needs around $1000 per month while on the trail to finance a hike. This proved to be about right for me. However, this can be reduced. One sure way of decreasing these expenses is to spend less time in towns. Get what you need and get back on the trail the same day. This will save on lodging expenses and restaurant meals.

In my younger days I would be more willing to pass on a nice comfy bed and long hot shower. I'm not so inclined these days, but if finances are tight it's the best way to reduce the cost of hiking long distance. But, be careful not to burn out. We all need a little down time once in a while. Getting a little R&R can be a big morale booster. This can be done on or off the trail. Some people take on-trail zero days (days of no hiking). Getting a rest day about once per week definitely helped me.

There were also expenses prior to the hike. These include purchasing gear, stocking and sending resupply boxes, and travel arrangements. I arranged for most of my resupply boxes to be delivered by friends. This saved on shipping, but also allowed me to keep in touch with my support system.

If a hiker needs but has not secured employment for after

the hike, add a couple months' worth of living expenses to the savings to cover the time it will take to land a job again.

The bottom line here is to be careful to plan the financial side of the adventure. Set your own financial comfort level and remember above all to plan for this time to be enjoyed. Don't add anything that will take that away.

Gear Prep

I'm a professional project manager by trade. I create plans and carry out plans for a living. I manage risks and navigate through obstacles that get in the way of achieving goals every day. I brought these skills to the table for my CT hike. Some may suggest that I might have been a little obsessive about it. Maybe I was. But it was a fun and rewarding exercise for me. Every gear choice was well-researched and intentional. I did side-by-side comparisons of multiple brands and models and considered all these options against factors that mattered to me. Weight, durability, cost, ratings, comfort, size, materials, functionality, features, and many other factors were considered for each item I carried.

I have provided my gear list in a later chapter of this book. This list isn't to suggest or recommend any product for anyone. I'm a strong advocate of everyone doing their own thing. Do what's important to you. Take the gear that you believe will make your hike safe and comfortable – or whatever criteria defines what is good for you. Avoid the gear-shaming people. Yes, hike your own hike.

Because I believe weight multiplied by miles is a formula that should not be ignored, I will often suggest that a thru-hiker buy the lightest option they can afford, that serves its function, and that makes them comfortable (enough). The toll that weight takes on the body, mind, and spirit while on the trail for weeks or months is the motivator behind making this an important factor.

Figure 2 - Colorado Trail gear

Shakedown Prep

A shakedown hike is a 3 to 10-day hike taken before the thru-hike. The intent is to test the person and the gear. The goal is to take yourself and your gear through all the likely scenarios that will come up on the trail. Cook with your stove, go through hygiene routines, pack and unpack, set up and tear down camp, make sure the shoes and socks are comfortable and don't cause blisters, test the rain gear, use your navigation tools, make sure clothing will be adequate, filter water, etc. Give it all a good run-through. Take good notes. Make appropriate adjustments when you return.

My Shakedown Hike

I did a 3-day shakedown hike in the Lost Creek Wilderness Area. This Wilderness Area is part of Segment 4 of the CT, maybe 10-15 miles southeast of Bailey, Colorado. It was a 38-mile excursion. I started at the Ute Creek Trailhead, connected with the Brookside-McCurdy Trail and followed Indian Creek until I reached Lost Park, which connects to the Wigwam Trail. Then I followed the Wigwam Trail to Goose Creek Trail until it intersected with the McCurdy Park Trail. This trail connects with a Brookside-McCurdy Trail, which took me back to the Ute Creek

Trail.

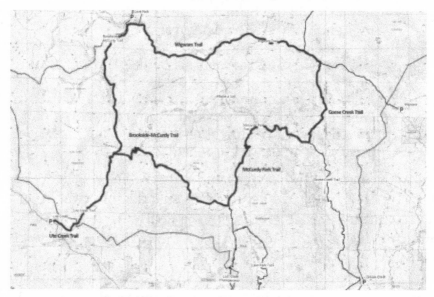

Figure 3 - My shakedown hike route in Lost Creek Wilderness

This hike was an average of 12.6 miles and 2640 feet of elevation gain per day. It was close to the planned average for my CT hike. I wanted to feel an average day. It also had comparable altitudes between 9000 and 11,500 feet. It was tough, as expected, because I don't plan on starting this way. I intend on gradually building up to this average when I get to the CT. It was a good mental workout too because I pushed myself beyond my comfort zone. There were so many advantages to doing a shakedown hike. Here is a short list:

- It informed adjustments to my physical workout routine.
- It showed me where I needed to make improvements to how I arranged the items inside and outside my pack.
- It gave me a chance to experience what meal prep and eating would be like on the trail.
- Practicing hygiene routines helped me adjust what I would bring to satisfy a certain level of cleanliness.

- I learned about my hiking cadence and how I might want to slow down my pace.
- I practiced how to find a good tent sight and put up my tent in different soils and settings.
- I learned more about foot care.
- I had a good round of mental training through the distance and elevation gains/losses.
- I gained some comfort with... here it is... pooping in the woods. A person does not want to be constipated out there. Get comfortable; it's your new home. I suppose one could say "the world is your toilet".

Unfortunately, I didn't get any rain or bad weather. I say "unfortunately" because I wanted to spend some time in the rain to test my gear and learn how to deal with less desirable conditions. I guess I would just have to figure that out on the CT. And I did.

It was hot, which was good to help me understand how to keep myself cool, how to deal with hydration levels, and to help me figure out how much water I should carry.

The Lost Creek Wilderness Area is a fantastic choice for a CT shakedown hike. And the icing on the cake is that it's a beautiful area. It gets a little crowded on the weekends here, but I did a mid-week hike, which aligned perfectly with my desire to get in a little isolation.

Figure 4 - Wigwam Trail, Lost Creek Wilderness

Figure 5 - Refrigerator Gulch - Lost Creek Wilderness Area

Figure 6 - - Near McCurdy Peak in the Lost Creek Wilderness Area

Figure 7 - Taken just below Bison Peak looking down at Indian Creek in the Lost Creek Wilderness Area - 10-Mile Range near Breckenridge on the horizon

Route Prep

Route planning is a worthy exercise, but not just for planning purposes. What route planning did for me was introduce me to the trail in a deeper, more intimate way. It's good to understand the available connections to towns, alternative routes, historic areas, must-see diversions, resupply options, emergency services, reliable water sources, elevation impact, exposure areas, terrain challenges, etc.

I planned my mileage and camp location for every single day. It was fun. It made me even more excited. And then on the first day of my CT hike it all changed. But that was expected, and I didn't care. I learned more about the trail, which gave me a greater appreciation and respect for what I was about to do.

I had planned my resupply stops and made hotel reservations. I mostly kept to those dates, but everything in between was negotiable. I didn't camp at many of the places I thought I would, and there were far more camp sites along the trail than what The Colorado Trail Databook indicated.

I did my route planning and general prep discussions with my buddy Larry (trail name: Pagosa). He and I met online and because we had so much in common, we eventually decided to start this trek together. It was good to bounce ideas off each other. Getting more people specifically involved, as mentioned earlier, is a way to build in accountability and ramp up the excitement and anticipation of the trail.

Our primary planning tool was a spreadsheet. The file had tabs for menu planning; gear by category with weights to include food, water (and other consumables), and worn items; an elevation profile of the trial that had itinerary markers; itinerary to include various calculations for miles, elevation, resupplies, costs, camp locations, and other notes; shakedown hike options; and resupply with item details per location/shipment. Since both of us are wired the same way about planning, it was like iron sharpening iron – definitely a fun exchange.

Food Prep

I'm a foodie. I can't help it. Bobbi is a fantastic cook, my youngest daughter runs a food blog, and my son-in-law is a trained chef. I've also adopted a much healthier life style over the years. I'm a pescatarian (a vegetarian that also eats seafood). Put all this together and it spells challenge for a thru-hiker. But

I found a way to overcome the challenge. I made my own meals for the trail.

Most people will resupply in towns, have prepacked meals sent to mail drops, or some combination of both. These are great options. Resupplying in towns encourages good relations between hiker towns and the hiking community. Prepackaged meals aren't cheap, but they are easy to prepare and far less hassle than preparing your own meals.

But, of course, I don't choose the easy way. I think I spent the better part of a several months dehydrating meals, creating protein bars and breakfast mixes, making meal plans, and all the minutia that goes along with that. Again, it was fun. I felt more in control of my calorie and nutrition intake. It was cheaper and my food variety was greater than if I had purchase prepacked foods. Here are a few of the entrees I dehydrated:

- Basil Walnut Penne in Cream Sauce
- Near East Couscous with Mushrooms
- Lentil Veg
- Mushroom Stroganoff
- Creamed Salmon on Potatoes
- Mushroom Risotto
- Ginger and Orange Bulgur with Veg
- Veggie Pasta Primavera
- Cheesy White Bean Veggies over Rice
- Cordoba Lentil Stew on Rice
- Moroccan Veggie Stew

I did leave about a third of my food for town resupplying. This way I felt better about giving back to these trail towns.

I planned for 2500-4000 calorie intake per day. I rarely consumed more than 3000 calories per day. It's just difficult to carry and eat that many calories.

The general idea is to take the most calorie-dense foods possible without sacrificing the enjoyment of good tasting food, while minimizing the weight. Find the balance that works for you. But no matter what food is brought on the trail, the hiker will eventually grow tired of "trail food" and end up taking what is desired, with lesser regard for caloric intake, nutritional value, or weight.

My advice with food planning is to prepare or buy maybe 30-50% up front for the first leg of the hike and resupply boxes with items that fit your palette and budget. The remaining is an allotment for changes in appetite and cravings on the trail that you can buy in resupply towns. You don't want to end up with a lot of food not eaten or tossed out along the way. If you stay in hostels, notice the type and amount of food hikers leave behind in hiker boxes; it's all that undesired food they didn't plan on hating. Leaving the food planning a little loose also fits into the theme of living a life that is little less tied to schedules and plans.

CHAPTER FOUR

And So It All Begins - Waterton Canyon to Breckenridge

A fter years of dreaming and months of planning my hike of the CT, the day had finally come. Pagosa and I took our first steps at 9am, July 15, 2018, from the north terminus at Waterton Canyon Trailhead just west of Denver, CO, almost 50 miles from Denver International Airport.

Figure 8 – Pagosa (right) and I starting the trail

Pagosa and his wife, Kristie, had stayed the night near my

home in Colorado Springs. We had dinner together the night before and talked about this long-awaited day. It would be our last non-dehydrated dinner until we reached Breckenridge eight days later. Kristie drove us to the trailhead in the morning, about an hour and a half from the house.

It was the most ideal start. It is normally a long, hot, 7-mile hike up the road to Strontia Springs Dam in July. But today clouds were blocking the sun and a cool wind was blowing down the canyon. We stopped briefly to talk with the ranger near the park entrance. We signed the log. It felt official now.

The ranger told us of bear sightings and how one bear had recently torn apart a tent to get to a power bar. There's always more to stories like that. I'm not sure if the absence of the whole story is intentional and part of a scare tactic to get people to behave in the wild, but it's close enough to what could be true for it to be believable.

He also asked us to watch out for the mountain sheep. Sure enough, a couple miles up the road a group of about 30 sheep were blocking our way. We enjoyed the delay long enough to take a few pictures before they made a way for us to pass.

Figure 9 – Sheep along the Waterton Canyon Road

There were rest stops with toilets and covered picnic tables every couple miles along the road. These were nice respites but precisely not what we should expect for the rest of the trail.

At one of the rest stops a young boy was playing when he was stung by a wasp. Pagosa and I broke out our first aid kits to no avail. The poor traumatized kid found little comfort in our gesture. His dad after exhausting his entire daddy playbook turned back to take the wounded home where surely Mommy would know how to make things better.

The road follows the South Platte River for 6.6 miles where it splits. One road was fenced off toward Strontia Springs Dam and the other a maintenance road that took us to where the trail became a single track.

Where the road splits we filled up our water supply (3 liters). We had been told earlier that normally running streams up the trail were dried up. It might be another 12 miles before we had another water source. In fact, it wasn't until mid-morning the next day before we arrived at our next water source.

Figure 10 - South Platte River along Waterton Canyon Road

Pro Tip: When filling up with water take the time

> to drink at least a half-liter while at the water source. It's a great way to hydrate without depleting personal water supplies, the supply that is carried will last longer, and normally less water will need to be carried.

At the single track there was mild rejoicing, as hikers like me are not fond of road walking, even if through a nice canyon. Being on a single track felt more like a trail. It was getting real.

Lenny's Rest came soon after. Lenny's Rest is a memorial bench with an engraving. Lenny was a young man, Boy Scout, who died in a hiking accident near here.

We began our first real ascent with switchbacks. There's not much for vistas along this part of the trail but the forest is thick and plush in the low areas. Wild raspberries were beginning to ripen on the vines. And as foretold, all runoffs and small creeks were dry, with the exception of a couple stagnant small pools near Bear Creek.

Just before Bear Creek, Pagosa spotted a young rattle snake on the trail. Apparently, I had walked right over it as I was not too far ahead of him. OK, so now I'm paying attention to where I put my feet!

My understanding about young rattle snakes is that they are more lethal than adult snakes because they don't yet know how to manage the release of their venom. A young snake will release all their venom, as opposed to an adult who will release a smaller controlled dose.

Figure 11 - Watch out for rattle snakes along the trail

Pro tip: Make no mistake, rattle snake bites are a medical emergency. If bitten take these steps: get away from the snake, take note of its size and color, and call for medical assistance immediately. Do not raise the bite area above or level with the heart, calm yourself to lower your heart rate, and do not try to hike back to get help. Let the wound bleed, do not wash it, don't cut the wound, don't try to suck the venom out, don't use a tunicate, and don't ice the wound. Place a loose bandage over the wound to keep dirt out. Left untreated, body functions will break down over a couple days with potential severe damage to organs and even death. So, this is serious stuff. (Elaine K. Luo 2017)

A light, steady rain began falling around 2pm. As we set up camp at mile 12.2 the fog thickened, and the rain had mostly stopped. This gave us a somewhat dry time to prepare dinner. We were joined in the same camp between the rocks by several other hikers.

On this, my first night on the CT, I drifted off to sleep to the light pitter patter of soft rain on my tent.

The rain stopped around 3am. I was up at 5am. I broke camp and had a quick breakfast. Nearly everything was wet or damp. But the sky was breaking, and the early sun was penetrating the forest. We would have some sun in our future.

Figure 12 - The first camp site along Segment 1

While spending most of my recent days and years sitting in an office, the sun was of far less consequence to my daily activities. We go about our days without giving much thought to whether the sun shines or hides behind clouds. But not out here. That celestial body is a life source having great consequence to every step of our day. Yesterday we exchanged its heat for a cool breeze and rain that would eventually make for some discomfort. But today would be different. Today the sun would have an opposite and equal effect.

We stopped at a nice overlook above the South Platte River a couple miles down the trail to dry our tents and other items on a rock outcrop in the morning sun. The fog lifting from the river valley below offered a nice morning view and it gave us a glimpse into our near future.

Figure 13 - The South Platte River Valley near the end of Segment 1

A few miles later we were down in that valley. I washed my feet and rinsed my socks in the river. The water was cold; toes numbed after a minute or so. We also filtered some water here as we entered Segment 2 and began our walk through the upcoming burn scar.

It did not rain today, there was not a cloud in the sky for most of the day. The burn scar would prove to be punishing and relentless. The Torture, as we affectionately called it, begins a short distance from the river. There are two large areas of this segment that are totally without shade, separated by some scantly wooded areas that brought only mild and temporary relief from the sun.

It was along this stretch we first met Talus and his dog Pablo. Talus was recording a video documentary of the CT for a school project. His pack was heavy with a full complement of video gear to include a drone. Pablo helped by carrying his own supplies in a very loosely fitting dog pack. He was a rescue dog, loyal as any dog could be and full of energy. They both took a siesta under some brush as Pagosa and I pressed on.

Despite the heat we decided to push 4 miles beyond our originally planned camp, partly because we were low on water but mostly because we didn't want to deal with the burn scar any more.

Toward the end of the scar we were treated with a nice view of Raleigh Peak and building thunder clouds. These clouds would later rush us to set up out tents.

Figure 14 - The burn scar of Segment 2 – A view of Raleigh Peak

At the border of the burn scar as we crossed Deckers Road we detoured one 10th of a mile to the generous offering of the local fire station: water. It's open to all thru hikers and bikers. A donation box gave us an opportunity to express our appreciation. Our newly quenched bodies ached but our spirits were happy to have all that behind us.

> **Pro Tip:** Some hikers will carry an umbrella for multiple purposes. It can keep you dry in the rain, of course. But it can also be used to provide shade in hot areas such as the burn scar. It's common to see umbrellas used in desert hiking, like the Arizona Trail and southern portions of the Pacific Crest Trail and the Continental Divide Trail. Some umbrellas don't do well in the wind and they can be troublesome if the hiker also needs trekking

poles and doesn't have a good way of securing the
umbrella to the shoulder straps.

Although the burn scar was not a friendly environment,
we met quite a few bikers and hikers with begrudged smiles
like our own. It made the day a little more tolerable knowing we were not alone in this. One hiker with a pack as full as
ours passed us at a jogger's pace, drenched in sweat. Whew! No
thanks. It was about then we sat and took a break.

Taking inventory for today: We met a biker family (parents
and two daughters), Talus and his dog Pablo, a young man from
Buena Vista, and an Army guy biking. I'll get more specific about
names later along the trail. As I became more familiar with the
trail community, I became more conversational and curious
about the people I met.

All this was enough for one day. We put in 15 miles with
3000ft elevation gain. We camped at mile 27.5. Day 2 was in the
books.

Figure 15 - Camp day 2

We had a beautiful setting for camp. I didn't pay much attention to it while setting up due to being rushed by the ap-

proaching thunder. But it turned out that it didn't rain and with both sides of my tent open, allowing the breeze to blow through, it was a very pleasant rest.

We broke camp and were on the trail by 6:45. Within the hour we ended Segment 2 and began Segment 3.

This would be a mild day compared to the one previous. The terrain was small rolling hills, mostly going around small ridges and dipping into small creek beds. All the small creeks on the map had a trickle of water.

We met up again with the friendly biker family as they were packing up their camp a couple miles from where we made camp. Later that morning after they had passed us again, we came across the mother and youngest daughter. The daughter had been in a minor bike accident; just below the knee was a gash that the mother was nursing. We went ahead to catch up to the father who then came back to help. We saw them later, all patched up with smiles again. That was good to see. And it's great to see families together out here.

Eight miles into Segment 3 we took a 90 min break to have lunch, rinse out our socks and shirts, and refill our water containers at Buffalo Creek. It was nice, refreshing.

It doesn't take long to notice how the forest transitions as we move further along the trail. One thing we noticed today was obvious forest maintenance activities. The Forest Service folks collect and stack dead fall for controlled burns they will do in the later winter months. This helps control the spread of forest fires by reducing the amount of materials that fuel the fires.

Figure 16 - Forest management for the upcoming winter controlled burn

In places like Colorado it's easy to seek out and anticipate the big vistas and grandiose views. And why not? After all, this is "Rocky Mountain High, Colorado". But those scenes are merely a conglomerate of smaller settings, portions of landscape, each contributing in their own way to the beauty that forms those magnificent panoramas. One of those moments of recognition came today as we rounded a bend in the path. It was a patch of Horsemint plants in full bloom. I literally stopped to "smell the roses (horsemint)" along the way. The trail, this country, is beautiful in many ways. And sometimes it's not the vistas that impress; it's the smaller things. It's when we realize the depth of its beauty.

Figure 17 - Horsemint edging the trail

As promised by the weather report, afternoon thunder storms rolled in. We left the creek after the first shower went over us and made it to our camp right about the time the second one hit.

Earlier in the day we had thought that maybe we could push further than scheduled like we did yesterday. But both of us were tired and thought that maybe we should take what remained of the afternoon to rest. Even with the 90-minute break, we were still weary from Segment 2.

In the beginning of a long trail like this, as I eluted to in the beginning chapters of this book, some good advice is to start off slow and build up to more difficult days. They will surely come. The idea is to gradually build and condition the body, mind, and spirit to avoid injury and to overcome the mental lows. Given our long walk through Segment 2, we weren't exactly following this advice and it was starting to reveal its truth. So, we rested.

I took a nap on a flat rock. Prior to today I had believed I could fall asleep just about anywhere. Today I proved even a rock is no challenge. While I rested on my comfy rock, Pagosa reclined on his camp chair in the shade.

We hung our clothes out to finish drying between showers, ate our dinners, send messages home, and prepped for the next day. At 7:30pm I was ready for a little reading, journaling, and surveying the day to come before calling it a night.

And now I'd like to pause so I can thank all the babies of the world. Without you, no one would have invented baby wipes. And without baby wipes us thru-hikers would not have a convenient way of cleaning up before bed, and probably wouldn't clean up nearly as often. So, thank you babies. And thank you Nice-Pak, the assumed inventor of baby wipes back in the 1950s.

Taking a nero (near zero – some hiking, but less than a full day) day to rest was good for us. The next day we felt more energy.

Day 4 was the day we first met Redbird and Kurt. Redbird is a fellow resident of Colorado Springs and Kurt is from Texas. Both had set out to hike segments of the CT. Redbird would end up finishing half the trail and Kurt finished up through the end of Segment 5 at Kenosha Pass. Redbird has plans to complete the trail next year and Kurt will be coming back as well to do the next five segments.

Over the course of the entire trail my estimation is that half of the people I met were either section or day hikers. It doesn't really matter how much of the trail a person does; there's no rules about hiking the entire distance, finishing what was planned, or how a person goes about piecing together what segments they do or when. The only true advice is to get out on the trail and do whatever can be done, whatever time allows, at whatever speed and distance seems right, or whatever the pocketbook can afford. Whatever is right for the person, do that. My parents would have said, "To each their own." In hiker lingo we say, "Hike your own hike."

Also, notice people's names on the trail are often not their given names. Many people use trail names. A trail name is a name of our choosing or it's a name given to us by fellow hikers while we are on the trail. It provides some anonymity and it further allows us to separate ourselves from our normal life. There is usually a story behind the name, which makes for good conversation and insight.

We passed a rifle range in Segment 3, where a sign was posted appropriately reminding us to stay on the trail. I think obvious advice like this is funny. It probably wouldn't say "Please stay off the trail" or if it did there would be a different set of risks to consider. Or it could say something like "Duck if you hear loud noises" – that would be interesting advice. No matter. We didn't hear any gunshots, but we did stay on the trail. So, it turned out to be good advice.

Figure 18 - The "Please Stay on Trail" plea

We also met Robot today whose work allowed him 6 weeks off to enjoy the trail. We met young and not so young, friendly and reserved; there are all kinds on the trail.

Today we entered our first Wilderness Area on the CT - The Lost Creek Wilderness Area. This is an area north and east of the area I had been in for my shakedown hike, mentioned earlier.

Finding a quality place to rest along the way is sometimes more challenging than it might first seem. Not every rock, log, or patch of earth is comfortable. We looked for what came to be known as furniture. Furniture could be a nice level log, stump, or rock that could be covered with a foam pad to make it "comfortable". All definitions of comfort are relatively adjusted for the environment.

> **Pro Tip:** Many hikers carry a foam pad to sit on during rest breaks. Mine is built into my Gossamer Mariposa pack as a back pad. It can be removed easily and repurposed. To save pack weight thru-hikers will have multiple purposes for many things they carry.

Figure 19 - Kurt took this of Pagosa (right) and I in Segment 4 - taking a rest on some nice furniture

After today I will have only one more full day of food to carry before our first resupply. The pack is noticeably lighter. The plan is to meet up with a friend, Ben, the morning after next with a three-day supply. This will last us to Breckenridge for our first zero day – a full day of no hiking.

Today was the actual day that Larry decided on his trail name. From here forward he was known as Pagosa. Mine was selected by me before the hike: David on Earth. It seemed convenient and fitting since I had adopted this name some time ago. The story is on my website of the same name: https://

www.davidonearth.com/.

The trail was very steep in some places today. There was a section in Segment 4 where the trial was nothing but loose rocks. A section that could be termed "Level 2 Fun". That is, a length of time not necessarily filled with smiles, but part of an overall time of enjoyment ranked better than being stuck in an office doing things that bring little real fulfillment.

There were few vista views today, but the forests were beautiful; it was quiet and peaceful. And the views as we approached camp were unmistakably Lost Creek.

Figure 20 - Lost Creek Wilderness Area

Camp was at 10,199 feet elevation, cooler than the previous night at 7900 feet. We all camped at the same general location along the north fork of Lost Creek. It was Pagosa, Kurt, Redbird, and me. There were a couple others in the same area we met along the way as well. We were at 9 miles into Segment 4. The total for the day was 12 miles and around 2700 feet elevation gain.

Before we left camp the next day we said so long to Kurt. He would be leaving camp a little later and we weren't sure we'd see him again.

Figure 21 - Kurt at camp along the North Fork of Lost Creek, Segment 4

This is the day we would finish the Lost Creek area and move into the Kenosha Range, where the excitement began to grow. We caught our first glimpse of the mountains ahead of us.

Figure 22 - Our first look at the mountains ahead of us

Tomorrow by noon we will get our resupply at Kenosha Pass and hike another few miles for a light day. But for today Johnson Gulch would be our destination.

One spectacular highlight of this day was hearing a bull moose call. I had heard such calls on other adventures, so it was unmistakably familiar. We didn't see the moose, but it was very close across Johnson Gulch and through some trees from our camp. The intentional snorts and grunts echoed across the way. We heard its hoofs pound the ground at it stomped its way through the trees, hidden from our view. It was quite amazing to witness. If only we had seen it. They are incredible creatures.

Figure 23 - Johnson Gulch camp

An hour or so before our moose call experience we saw what looked like a huge black bear about a quarter mile down the gulch. We didn't get a close enough picture to confirm. For a time, we suspected that it might have been a cow, as some black cows showed up in the gulch shortly after that. But it was later confirmed by another hiker; indeed, it was a bear, a large one.

> **Pro Tip:** There's lots of misinformation out there about bear safety. So, take advice from bear biologist, Tom Smith. Here are a few tips: bear spray is better than guns but don't spray it around your tent because it doesn't work like bug repellant, make appropriate noises, avoid hiking alone, keep your distance, stand your ground, don't turn your back and run away, don't smell yummy, don't

bring banana-colored tents, store food properly, and don't play dead with a black bear. (Alvarez 2017)

Today I long for a shower. Washing in a creek and using baby wipes is proving to be inadequate for me. I'm not yet embracing the "hiker trash" odor. In a few days we'll be in Breckenridge. My body is excited about that.

Thoughts of food on a plate were starting to creep into our conversation. I knew the day would eventually come when I would start craving a meal that didn't need to be rehydrated. Now, with less than a week into the trail we started talking about what our town meal would be. Pagosa was ready for a spicy burger. I was a little less discriminate; anything I didn't need to spoon out of a bag was good for me. And, of course, a nice cold beer would need to be considered.

Before closing my eyes, I took one long final look at the scenery around us. It's a wondrous world and I'm blessed to be right here, right now. It's peaceful, quiet, exactly what I came out here to receive.

Today we completed Segment 4 and hiked 8.4 miles of Segment 5 for a total of 16.1 miles and a modest 1700-foot elevation gain.

We were up with the sun again the next morning. Following the sun seems to be the pattern; laying down as the sun does and getting up as the sky brightens. It's simple and natural.

We had cows on the trail this morning. They were quite messy and boisterous. I'm starting to learn their behavioral patterns. When and how they sound off is distinct to the time of day and activity.

Today would be my first experience with a trail angel. Trail Angel's bring magic. Magic is unexpected goodness, like soda, cold water, fresh fruit, an offer to take trash, give out candy, offer a ride, or any other act of kindness to bring a smile to face or belly. And sometimes it's quite serendipitous. Anyone can be a trail angel and trail angels can do their work anywhere.

Michelle was our angel today. She brought us fresh fruit and sodas and offered to take our trash. She was there to support a couple: Silver and Turtle. We would connect again with those two a little further down the trail. Yeah, Michelle!!

Also, at Kenosha Pass, Ben brought us our resupply. Yeah, Ben!!

Regretfully, I have no pictures of Michelle or Ben.

The hike into Kenosha Pass has several expansive panoramic views that overlook nearly the entire South Park and have the Ten Mile and Mosquito Ranges as the skyline on one side. On the other side is Bison Peak and other high points of the Lost Creek Wilderness Area.

Figure 24 - Our view from the Kenosha mountains looking toward South Park

It seems each forest we've walked through has had its own character. One today was a mature Aspen forest, part of which had been burned by a fire in recent years. These aspens tower dozens of feet into the air and shade us with their high canopy.

Figure 25 - Kenosha Pass aspen forest

Redbird caught up with us at the Pass. We enjoyed the trail magic together. He needed to wait for his brother and would later meet us at camp a few miles up the trail.

We refilled our water at Kenosha Pass Campground West. Someone had told us the campground host gets a little grumpy with us thru-hikers using the water pump to get water. We did not find these stories to be true. We pumped our water in peace without any gruff from the good man. Yeah, campground host guy!!

Guernsey Creek is our camp for the night. We had a nice big open camping area, and the creek was running very good and clear compared to Johnson Gulch and a few other recent creeks.

We met up with Talus and Pablo again at camp. He had some Achilles heel issues and decided to take an on-trail zero to recover. We hoped he could join us tomorrow morning.

The talk around dinner was that we all noticed and acknowledged our body odor. It's part of the deal. But today I did something about it. After setting up my tent at camp I immediately took out my bottle of soap and introduced it to my bandana. They teamed together to wash my stinky self. I also washed the wool shirt I had worn since the beginning of the hike. Merino wool is especially good at absorbing moisture and fending off odor, but it can only take so much before it needs a wash. We made a clothesline from some thin twine and let the clothes dry overnight.

Today we finished Segment 5 and hiked 3.1 miles of Segment 6.

Figure 26 - Kenosha Pass sign near the trailhead

We were up again at the crack of dawn. Last night the temperature dipped down to 37 degrees. I wore a couple layers, anticipating it would get chilly. In the morning there was some condensation in the tent and the outside was still a little wet from the rains. The clothes on the line had not dried as we had hoped. I wiped down my tent the best I could, but it was still a little damp when we arrived at camp later that day.

As I was breaking camp, I noticed some unusual clouds. These were wispy and followed the course of the skyline. They were darker, dirty looking. I later understood that this was smoke in the atmosphere from fires burning in Colorado and in other western states. We had smelled smoke along these early parts of the trail. It wasn't strong, but it was noticeable.

We were on the trail at 7:30am with a plan of deciding at

Georgia Pass about where we would camp for the night. It would depend on the weather and how we felt about our advancement for the day.

A field of morning flowers brightens the day.

Figure 27 - Aspen Sunflower

Figure 28 - Mariposa Lily

There were dozens of mountain bikers on the trail today, easily outnumbering hikers 4:1. Increased trail activity is a sign that it's the weekend, if you even care to know what day it is. I've grown sour over sharing the trail with so many non-hikers. Most of the bikes and even motor bikes assume the right of way, which is dangerous. Not all, but some of them act like they own the trail and unashamedly so. The rules of the trail suggest that those on foot have the right of way. (Schreiner 2018) I suppose I shouldn't be troubled by the multi-use of a multi-use trail. It's just the constant interruption of cadence gets to be annoying after a while. I wasn't the only annoyed hiker. I witnessed one hiker not move for bikers until they stopped and asked for permission to pass. I understand why he would do that, but it seems a bit too much. It's a shared trail. For the few that don't seem to care much about rules and common courtesy, can we just pause for a minute, look around to appreciate that we are sharing a wonderful place, and decide to be a little friendlier and more respectful? OK... that's all I want to say about that.

The big attraction today was Georgia Pass. And beautiful it was. We climbed to our highest point so far, 11,874 feet. And shortly after reaching the Pass we joined with the Continental Divide Trail (CDT), where we will remain for the next 314 miles. Essentially how this works as we head south is that the water in all creeks to our left will end up in the Atlantic and all to the right will end up in the Pacific. That's pretty cool!

Figure 29 - Georgia Pass

On the way up the pass we were met with approaching bad weather, so we had to rush our way through. I had hoped we could spend more time there, but it isn't smart to test these things. Lightning kills up here. So, we took a few pics on the top of the pass and moved along.

We arrived at camp around 4:30pm where the trail intersects with the Middle Fork of the Swan River.

Figure 30 - Middle Fork of the Swan River

There are lots of old metal pieces laying around, mostly from the mining days I suppose. And I've heard it can be a bit noisy being next to the county road (354). But it wasn't bad for us. We were content with this spot.

One item of note is that the variety of forest types so far has been impressive and somewhat mystical in places.

Figure 31 - Some places have lush green forest floors

Redbird continued to develop more blisters. His brother, a former corpsman treated him at Kenosha Pass yesterday and gave him some additional first aid supplies. He'll move slower, but I think he's on the mend.

We met up with a young couple we had seen earlier on the trail. It's always nice to reacquaint with fellow hikers. I didn't get their names. We also met a lady who started the same day we did. She tried to keep up with some younger folks but couldn't and injured both her feet in the process. A lesson in "hike your own hike".

> **Pro Tip:** Keeping up with a group of people is tempting and sometimes there's this competitive undertone among hikers. Avoid it all. Focus on *your* pace. Focus on *your* hike. You'll meet up with others soon enough and many times you'll meet up again with those who were ahead of you. It's often said that in thru-hiking "last place wins". So, save the trouble and just be you.

My shoulder blades and mid back have been tender and sore. I've managed to adjust my hiking to help the matter. And some ibuprofen helps. But what eventually ended up fixing this issue was a different size pack. My torso length is in the gray area between medium and large sized packs. I had a medium sized pack on the CT. A few weeks after the CT I was using a large size and the pain seems to have gone, but I've not been as taxed as I was on the CT. More time will tell.

I really like my hammock, but because of the weight and some places on the trail where it's not great for hammocks, I chose to bring an ultralight tent. But the thing with tents is that it can be difficult to find a flat spot. Last night it was difficult. So, I took out my small spade and made a flat spot by leveling off some small mounds and filling in some holes. I had not yet learned to tolerate a less-than-ideal sleeping spot. It would come later.

We made it to mile 17.1 of Segment 6 today, 89 miles so far!

It's now July 22nd. This day would be the day that we reached the 100-mile point on the trail. We would also head into Breckenridge a day early! The pessimist might say that we have 385 miles left to go. But it's a good feeling to have 100 miles down, a great milestone!

Figure 32 - Reaching the 100 mile point on the trail

I left camp before the others this morning. Shortly after leaving I heard what sounded like a big pack of coyote or wild dogs. I wasn't sure if I should wait for the guys to catch up or to proceed with caution. I chose the first option. Soon the guys caught up and one of them recalled a dog kennel along the trail. They train sled dogs at this kennel and they are quite rambunctious. So, on we went.

Along the trail today as our minds wondered as they often do, we were reminded of this weird guy camping near us the night before. He said he had been on the trail a while - like a couple hundred miles. Funny thing was that he wasn't dirty, he was clean shaven, his clothes looked fresh, he said he hadn't stayed in nearby Breckenridge, and he couldn't recall without some help where he had started from. He had a strange demeanor too, quite odd. As friendly as this trail is, it's still good to be cautious and aware.

We went through another burn scar area today. This was much smaller than Segment 2 and not nearly as harsh. We also hiked through a clear-cut area - the Forest Service intentionally does this to help slow the growth of future fires.

Figure 33 - Another burn scar area

We met a few guys from Big Agnes (gear) who were hiking the CDT. The story is that the whole company is out hiking the CDT in Colorado this summer. They are doing it in tag teams - actually carrying a baton to pass along to the next team. And along the way they are handing out power bars from their sister company: Stinger. It's a great snack for honey lovers. Good for us!

Figure 34 - Big Agnes hiking the CDT this summer

The views are getting better!

Figure 35 - The mountains are getting closer as we near Breckenridge

We decided to hike into Breckenridge a day early, ending Segment 6. We got a motel room about three miles from the trail head; the Wayside Inn. That last few miles of paved road walking put an exclamation point on the day. We could have saved half the walking by catching the bus from Revette Drive to Tiger Road, but we didn't know about the bus stops at the time. The Inn wasn't a five-star hotel but compared to sleeping on the ground and being without a shower for a week, one could say it was a place of luxury. It was clean, the staff was very accommodating, and it came at a price that fit a backpacker's budget, at least for a place like Breckenridge. The hot shower and (pricey) pizza were great!! Getting the layers of dust and sweat off the body refreshes the spirit. I washed my trail clothes in the shower. The fan in the room helped dry them overnight. Fresh trail clothes – what a treat!

Figure 36 - Breckenridge below!

Arriving at Breckenridge was a big milestone for us amateur thru-hikers. It seemed that we had crossed a threshold, that we had taken the first big step toward earning the right to be part of the thru-hiking community. There were many more days ahead, greater challenges yet to overcome, bigger views to take in, and more incredible experiences to log along our way to becoming a thru-hike finisher. We were feeling accomplished but ready for a zero day.

CHAPTER FIVE

Breckenridge to the Collegiate West

A rriving in Breckenridge a day early welcomed the idea of a nice 2-day rest, instead of the one day we had scheduled. But, as I will explain next, this wasn't meant to be.

A couple days before arriving at Breckenridge, Pagosa was experiencing ever increasing pain in his shins. "Shin splints", we thought. His leg started to swell, and his limp became delicate. The day after we arrived, he was able to see a doctor. The diagnosis turned out to be stress fractures. With a recovery time of weeks, sadly, his time on the trail had come to an end.

Of course, it's easy to say that he didn't have an option. But with as much preparation and planning that went into this and with a real sense of dreams dashed, letting go after only 100 miles didn't come easy and it didn't seem fair, it's tough to leave the trail like this. The mind races for alternatives; but there are none. Pagosa put on a good face, but I know that if it was me, I would not be able to contain my disappointment. He has vowed to finish the trail in the coming years, perhaps segment hiking. Kristie would pick him up in the morning.

With Pagosa out, I had the timing of my departure to consider. I could go on as planned, or I could get back on the trail with Redbird the next day. I phoned Bobbi with the situation and asked her if she would feel comfortable with me heading out solo. She felt that leaving with Redbird would make her more comfortable. So that was my decision; I would leave with Redbird in the morning. By then is was late in the afternoon. Instead of making a run to the grocery store to finish my resupply, Pagosa let me take what he had in his resupply box.

There was also a matter of figuring out my resupplies down the trail. Kristie had planned on doing many of those resupplies and had intended on still doing them even if Pagosa had to drop out for any reason. Bobbi and I talked through some logistics and I released Pagosa and Kristie from the obligation, but they insisted – a promise is a promise. The heart and integrity of these good people is enormous. He went from thru-hiker to trail angel, just like that.

Fortunately, I did get in a couple hot, glorious showers and we had a nice hearty lunch in town – with a local brew, of course. Along with my resupply box and Pagosa's generosity I had enough for me to finish packing.

> **Pro Tip:** High amounts of processed sugars like candy bars are not healthy options on or off trail. Take a break from the junk food for a day while you are in town and carry fresh foods out of town like hard boiled eggs, apples, cucumbers, avocados, bread, etc. Things that need refrigeration will normally last a day or two.

We caught the first bus out in the morning. It stops a short distance from the trailhead. Breckenridge and Frisco have a free bus service – pretty sweet! I was back on the trail with Redbird by 7:30am. Silver and Turtle were starting out at the trailhead that morning too. They had spent a couple days in Breck with a friend.

Figure 37 - Trailhead going south in Breckenridge

A few miles up the trail was another burn area. This one was more recent.

Figure 38 - A fresh burn scar... and the creek flows not bothered by the whole thing and ready to help rebuild.

Some portions of the trail were steep and long. Our highest elevation for the day was 12,500 feet. We rose above tree line for a good portion of the day. The views were spectacular from within the Tenmile Range. The trail rose to the saddle near Peak 6. This is ski territory in the winter.

The trail then descended very steeply to the town of Copper. It's a ski resort town.

Figure 39 - Starting the ascent out of Breckenridge

Figure 40 - Breaking above tree line after a steep climb

Figure 41 - Ten Mile Range up close

Figure 42 - The top of every climb is a celebration - this is the Peak Six saddle

Figure 43 - Silver (left) and Turtle taking a quick break on the saddle

Figure 44 - Copper mountain ski resort within sights

Redbird moved ahead of me while we were above tree line; he's not very fond of alpine areas. In these areas a person is exposed to the elements and storms can move in quickly. I typically like to spend time up high if I'm comfortable with what's going on in the sky. For me it's invigorating. It's like I can taste the freedom of the mountain. And the views on a day like this day were spectacular. But clouds were building so I didn't stay long.

I later caught up with Redbird, rested a while with him under some pines just below tree line, then moved on toward camp. The skies were darkening, and we could see rain off in the distance.

Before I left our resting spot among the pines, I took a picture of some subalpine Arnica. Arnica is a natural herb with yellow flowers. This plant is used as a pain reliever and it is also known to reduce swelling. (Arnica 2018) Naturalists caution against disturbing their root system because the plant is fragile and difficult to grow. (Ethical Harvesting of the Arnica Flower 2018)

Figure 45 – Subalpine Arnica herb among the pines

Along the way I talked with a young lady who was on her way back to Denver after completing the Collegiate Loop. That is, she started at Waterton Canyon, looped around the Collegiate Mountains (what I'm about to get into in a few days), and then back to Waterton Canyon. It's about the same distance as the CT thru-hike. The route she took was likely because some of the CT was closed near Durango when she started due to forest fires in that area. Maybe she decided on this alternate hike. She also gave me tips on how to deal with the ankle soreness I've been having. I didn't get her name or picture.

Redbird and I camped near the banks of Tenmile Creek. We arrived shortly after 3pm right about the time a thunderstorm was rolling in. Again, I rushed to set up the tent, but only a few sprinkles fell. This camp site is near Highway 91. The creek dampened the sound of the traffic and civilization.

While setting up camp another thru-hiker walked by. We talked briefly as he seemed to be driving hard to get to his camp for the night somewhere from where we had been earlier in the day. He was a CDT hiker who had started in the southwest desert of New Mexico at the border with Mexico earlier in May. He was on his way to Canada. And today was his birthday! Having now been on the trail for 10 days I was just beginning to understand this thru-hiking life. And to see one who had a much longer and tougher journey behind and ahead of him still going strong was encouraging and inspirational. I admire such stamina and endurance for the sake of a grand experience such as this. I wished him a happy birthday and cheered him on as he quickly went on his way.

Today was the most challenging day so far. We climbed approximately 3700 feet and nearly 13 miles into Segment 7.

> **Pro Tip:** There are tough days and hardships in thru-hiking. Expect it. Although I never thought about quitting, many people do. The advice from those more experienced has been to never quit on a bad day because a great day is ahead. Another good thing to remember is that a bad day on the trail is better than a good day in the office.

The night was easy and restful. Rising, eating, and breaking camp was starting to become an efficient process. I was on the trail before Redbird with a promise to meet him up the trail later in the day.

I like being alone on the trail in the morning. For me it's the most peaceful time of the day. It's fresh, new, and undisturbed.

The first part of the trail goes through the Copper Mountain Ski Area with a view of the town below. I had briefly considered a hot breakfast, but it didn't look like any businesses were open and I was enjoying a morning without interruption.

Figure 46 - Copper Mountain Resort below the trail

The trail was nicely maintained and crossed over a few run-off streams. There's nothing like cold, fresh mountain water.

Figure 47 - Jacque Creek

Just before Jacque Creek I passed a couple of older gentle-men, both grey and weathered with impressive beards, fully geared for life in the woods. "Mountain men", I thought. One was telling a story to the other so intently that pausing for a moment to return my greeting would have broken his auditory streaming. I didn't press it. The second man smiled and nodded in response to my well wishes. They moved on without pause.

Searle Pass was the first milestone of the day. The views up to the pass were worth a few pictures and an occasional pause to take it in. The trail would gain 2500 feet before the pass and so perhaps a break for any reason would be warranted.

Figure 48 - A minor mountain along the trail to Serle Pass

Figure 49 - A creek and several ponds along the way to Searle Pass

Figure 50 - Another spectacular view along the way to Searle Pass

Janet's cabin can be seen along the way. It's one of several remote mountain cabins that can be rented via www.huts.org. It's right near tree line (I don't have a picture). And after achieving tree line it would be several hours before we dropped into the trees again.

I sat on a rock outcropping near tree line to eat a snack. Redbird caught up with me about the same time as a small group of family and friends who were taking a day hike. It wasn't long before they decided to turn around and not risk the building weather danger.

Several bikers also passed us. They made it up to the pass, turned around, and headed back down. They too were not fond of the developing weather.

I filtered some water where Guller Creek crossed the trail and shortly after it started to rain. It was icy cold and windy. This lasted until a few minutes before I reached the top of Searle Pass.

The view from Searle Pass was worth the climb. But the wind and rain would return in waves to force us to move along the alpine terrain without time to linger for fear of worsening conditions.

Figure 51 - Searle Pass looking south

Kokomo Pass was the next waypoint; it was immediately after Elk Ridge. Elk Ridge was windy and wet. But as soon as I was on the other side the wind died down and the rain stopped.

Figure 52 - Elk Ridge in the rain

Figure 53 - Kokomo Pass

The plan was to do 16 miles, but when we arrived at our planned camp along Cataract Creek we were immediately swarmed by hundreds of flies from the pit of hell. They were intolerable. There was no way we could camp there. And I noticed no one else did either. The next potential camp was at least four miles ahead. Our options were limited, so we moved on.

Our next stop was Cataract Falls. It was tempting to get under the falls, but the water was quite cold.

Figure 54 - Cataract Falls

We were now entering Camp Hale, a World War II training ground for the 10th Mountain Division. The old bunkers are the main attraction here.

Figure 55 - Camp Hale bunkers

There's some road walking through here, and it's a flat. This area has enough unexploded ordinances in the ground that it's deemed too dangerous to wonder off trail or to camp in the area. We climbed up hill from the bunkers in search of a place to camp for the night.

We grew weary after a couple more miles and focused on finding a place to set up our tents, get some food in us, and crash for the night. The camping spot wasn't ideal, but good enough. I had no more energy to be selective about the flattest spot and the choices were again limited.

Overall, it was a very scenic day! And it was my first 20-mile day. What's that? Oh, OK. My feet just told me it will be my last 20-mile day. So, there you go.

The next two days should be much easier.

Pro Tip: Stretch frequently. It's easy to not do this because you're tired. But your calves, quads, back, and hamstrings will thank you. Stretch in the morning, during breaks, and before you crash at night.

I took my time getting to the trail the next morning, but not too late - 7:20.

Just a mile out of camp I came across a Boy Scout troop from Florida hiking a few segments of the CT. I gave them our story about the nasty flies at Cataract Creek and what to expect in the coming miles. One young man was intent on telling me of his great courage and experiences as a hiker. I smiled and wished them all a memorable adventure.

It was a short 2 miles before crossing highway 24.

Figure 56 - Crossing Highway 24

A short climb later the trail led to an abandoned railroad grade. I followed this for a few miles. Along the way I took out my rain coat to dry in the sun; it was still damp from the day before.

Figure 57 - Old railroad grade on the way to Tennessee Pass

On down the trail a bit were the remains of some old coking ovens. After some research I learned that coke ovens are used to transform coal into metallurgical coke through a process called dry distillation. The ovens are free of oxygen so they don't burn the coal; they burn off harmful by-products so the coal (now coke) can be used in blast furnaces to produce the heat required for liquefying metal. That's probably more than you ever wanted to know about how coal is prepared to be used in blast furnaces.

Figure 58 - Remains of an old coking oven

Tennessee Pass was the next stop. They had toilets; this was good. It's also where one can find a memorial to the 10th Mountain Division. This marked the end of Segment 8.

Figure 59 - Tennessee Pass WWII 10th Mountain Division Memorial

A half mile up the trail from Tennessee Pass is a wooden swing. Of course, I had to stop. It was delightful.

Figure 60 - A swing in the woods

The remainder of the trail today was a series of ups and downs with a creek at the bottom of each. Some creeks were dry.

What I continue to enjoy is the diversity of the forests... some dry, some with plush green floors, some dark and spooky.

We met a couple young men a few miles before our camp for the day. They were on break from school. I think it's fantastic that they would find the CT worthy of a summer break. No partying; instead, the freedom of the trail. It's a great place to check yourself, review intentions, secure some undisturbed time for reflection and direction setting. One of them was Baine, the other was his brother. I later hiked a few Segments with Baine. Great guy - more on him later.

Our camp for the night had a fantastic view of some mountains here in the White Water National Forest. We stopped here instead of going higher to Porcupine Lakes, which I'm told is fantastic as well. We shall see tomorrow morning.

We made it to mile 150 - Longs Gulch, mile 6.9 of Segment 9. Segment 8 is behind us. I'm still hiking with Redbird.

Figure 61 - Camp at mile 150

As we were settling for the night the skies didn't quite clear as usual. The air remained cool and humid.

We woke to condensation and dampness inside and outside the tent. I just want to get moving on this kind of morning, so I can warm up. I was out of camp by 6:30 and headed 500 feet up to Porcupine Lakes. I put on my rain gear due to the amount of moisture in the air. Only one of the lakes could barely be viewed from the trail because of the fog. But it made a great moment for photographers!

Figure 62 - Porcupine Lakes

Figure 63 - The morning sun trying to burn off the thick fog

Soon I rose above the fog to see a gorgeous view of the valley shrouded in the fog below. Galena Mountain and the surrounding hills were now islands in a white sea. In the most literal sense of the word: awesome!

Figure 64 - Fog fills the valley as I rise above it all

Figure 65 - A view of the mountains we had been in a few days before - the hills now islands in the fog

The trail undulates, reaching a high point of 11,716 feet, then dropping down to a group of lakes, among them: Galena and Bear Lakes. We would meet several fishermen coming up to the lakes to enjoy a quiet day wetting their lines.

Figure 66 - Galena Lake

The trail climbs again to one more saddle before descending two miles to the ending trailhead for the day.

> **Pro Tip:** The last thing you should do after taking a break or stop to filter water is to check the area to make sure you didn't leave any trash or gear behind. Leave no trace.

Figure 67 - One last saddle before descending to Turquoise Lake and ending the day

We would finish Segment 9 at Timberline Lake Trailhead near Turquoise Lake at mile 156.6. I'll be taking a zero day in Leadville and staying at the summer home of a friend of a friend. Redbird has reservations at a hotel just a few blocks up the road from me where he'll meet his wife.

Pagosa and Kristie made the several hour trip to pick us up and take us to lunch at High Mountain Pies... very yummy food... pizzas and sandwiches. They also brought me a set of trekking poles that Gossamer Gear wanted me to test for them.

The caretaker of the home I stayed at offered to take me to the trailhead on Sunday. This guy is trail angel material!

The trail is renewing my view of humanity. In the all too often selfish and dog-eat-dog world, I am seeing and experiencing the good in people. While the world is frantically and viciously fighting over religious and political differences, a stranger offers a place for me to stay the night and a friend gives up a weekend to drop off a resupply and provide transportation and a meal. Perhaps the hope of a positive future for humanity is grounded in a spirit that freely gives and sacrifices for others without regard for what they believe, who they love, or what political leanings they have.

The next day I spent a zero in Leadville. Cool town, literally; it's above 10,000 feet and stays cool even in the summer months. I love the vibe of this town – laid back, friendly, accommodating – yes, very cool!

Bobbi came out to see me. What a treat! We walked the half-mile main street and ate lunch at the Mexican restaurant. There was a biking event in town that weekend, so the few restaurants in town were full. Leadville Outdoors and Mountain Market had the fuel I needed and had a good selection of replacement gear for backpackers. We stopped at Safeway for a few more resupply items. My food carry would be a 7-day supply to get me through to Monarch Pass. That's around 11 pounds of food. I would be starting off heavy but by the time I start the Collegiate West I will be down to around 8 pounds of food. After doing some laundry and repacking I was ready for the trail again.

Figure 68 – Leadville

Figure 69 - Old mining towns have a great character

Calling something a "zero" day when I spend all day walking around town doing errands doesn't lend to the idea of a "rest" day. But it was good to shower, get something different to eat, and spend the day with Bobbi for sure!

Bobbi dropped me off at the trailhead the next morning. We waited a few minutes for Redbird, I said my goodbyes, and off I went into the woods again.

We've said many goodbyes over the years as I've traveled for work. But it's different when it's for something like this - a personal choice rather than a professional obligation. It takes a toll, knowing I've put my wife in a situation where she's alone and handling everything while I'm away for the sake of my personal goals. It's not that she can't handle it; she's quite independent and strong. But she's made it known that she doesn't understand why anyone would do a hike like this. She tries her best to understand that this trek has a significant and personal meaning and purpose for me. That she doesn't protest and that she is supportive as only a wife of 36 years can be... this encourages me to dig deep and to be sure that my reasons are at least as substantial as her dedication to me. And so, I must complete this and come out of this as a better me - a better father and husband. If I don't, I feel this whole thing would have been a selfish and hollow venture. The work I'm doing here is substantial - mentally, physically, emotionally, and spiritually.

I didn't take many pictures today; it was an introspective type of day. I was in my head a lot. It happens.

The trail followed the eastern foothills of Mount Massive, the second highest peak in Colorado. We caught brief glimpses of the mountain, but we were mostly hidden from it all day.

Figure 70 - Entering the Mount Massive Wilderness Area

We met a couple going by the name of Two Bad Dogs. The name, Two Bad Dogs, came from the fact that like dogs who are told to stay home, they just run off to their next adventure... but eventually go home again. They are a retired couple hiking the CDT. By September they will have completed the Triple Crown of thru hiking. That is, they hiked the Appalachian Trail, The Pacific Crest Trail, and the Continental Divide Trail – around 7000 miles of hiking! Next year they will be hiking a trail in Europe. They were adventurous, loving life, energetic, and encouraging. Nice couple! Inspirational!

We talked gear, trail conditions, and what life events lead us all to meet on the trail this day. This is what I love about the trail: it's all kinds of people; it's all different reasons; it's all good stories with diverse but unobjectionable perspectives; it's where humans can find substantial similarities and single-mindedness within such diversity. It's where people can actually and truly just get along.

Figure 71 - Two Bad Dogs

The weather was as could have been predicted... sunny morning with clouds in the afternoon. We had some sprinkles but nothing substantial.

I took the opportunity to wash myself and rinse out my socks near one of the creeks today - that's always nice. I'm growing accustomed to cold washes. It's refreshing, no doubt.

> **Pro Tip:** I had two pair of socks. I put on clean socks every morning. The dirty ones I rinsed in a creek then hung them on the outside of my pack using safety pins. The water got the dirt off, which prolongs the life of the sock, and the sun's UV rays helps kill the bacteria (which causes stinky feet/socks/shoes).

We camped near Halfmoon Creek not far from the trailhead to Mount Massive. We met a dozen or so people who had summited Mount Massive earlier in the day; they were tired and thinking the trailhead should be closer. I know what that feels like; the last mile is always the longest. It reminded me of the conversation I had with my peak-bagging friend, Brian: would I be able to do long days consecutively for weeks on end? The answer is a resounding "Yes, I can and I'm doing it!"

Figure 72 - We camped near here, the end of Segment 10

I completed Segment 10 today; it was 13 miles and 2700 feet of elevation.

It was here, the next morning, I would say so long to Redbird. He was leaving later that morning for a short day, staying the night at a hotel in Twin Lakes before continuing on the Collegiate East route. I would have a longer hiking day today, finishing Segment 11 and then starting into the Collegiate West alternate route. I would be solo for the first time on the hike.

From the Mount Massive trailhead, I crossed County Road 110 and quickly connected with the (northeast ridge) Mount Elbert trail. It would ascend a few switch backs before splitting.

The CT would turn left, the trail to Mount Elbert to the right.

A few young folks passed me along the way. I tried making small talk about what I assumed was their attempt at Mount Elbert, but it was met with only a couple snippy remarks and childish giggles. Like I said, the trail has all kinds, mostly friendly but there are a few that didn't get the memo about being a nice and respectable person. I suspect I may have looked like someone who had been spending the past couple weeks in the woods, which can prompt different types of reactions. There is a noticeable difference between how thru-hikers interact with each other and how occasional day hikers interact with thru-hikers. Thru-hikers get thru-hikers. I was happy about taking a left at the intersection.

Before reaching the next intersection, the south trailhead for Mount Elbert, there are beaver ponds. In fact, as one might expect from the tallest peak in Colorado, there is plenty of water in the run-off creeks in this area.

Figure 73 - Plenty of water below Mount Elbert

Looking to the right of the trail one is teased with brief views of the upcoming Collegiate Peaks.

Figure 74 - Mountains tease

Figure 75 - South trailhead to Mount Elbert

From the south trailhead to Mount Elbert the trail descends toward Twin Lakes. There are several cascading streams along the way. I stopped at one to notice I had cell reception, so I phoned Bobbi. A few minutes later I had my first glimpse of Hope Pass, the first big climb of the Collegiate West, which I would take on tomorrow.

Figure 76 - Descending down to Twin Lakes. Ringer Peak in the foreground, Hope Pass left center

The highlight of the day was the trek around Twin Lakes. The purest in me would not allow the shorter off-CT route connecting the CT to Willis Gulch Trailhead, just west of Twin Lakes (the village). Some might find circumnavigating Twin Lakes less appealing because of the heat and the slog. I don't. It's part of the whole experience. What makes the greatness of the trail is its variety of character; its highs and lows. Taking the hike around the lake presents part of this uniqueness. The trail goes under a road, the only time it does. One of only a few dams is crossed along this route. And it's the only sandy beach along the trail. So, why not take this route?

Figure 77 - The trail goes under Highway 82

Figure 78 - Sage brush trails toward sandy beaches

Figure 79 - Sandy beaches

Figure 80 - south shore Twin Lakes

I sat for a quick break along the south shore of the lake before taking on the final portion of my hike today, toward Interlaken and then taking on one more ascent. It would be my official start to the Collegiate West alternative route.

Another milestone was in the bag as I placed my feet at the start of the Collegiate West. Behind me is are the ski resort towns of Breckenridge and Copper Mountain, the historic Camp Hale, the wonderful Mount Massive Wilderness Area, and Twin Lakes. Ahead of me is one of the most rugged portions of the trail with expansive alpine vistas, crystal blue lakes, and one of the most isolated experiences of the trail, the Collegiate West route.

CHAPTER SIX

The Collegiate West

A bout a mile short of the Interlaken Historical Site on the south shore of Twin Lakes the trail splits between the Collegiate East and West routes. The sign is easy to miss, as it's set back from the trail a few feet. I met a couple of hikers that missed it and needed to backtrack. The look on their faces as they realized they were on the wrong trail was soooo familiar. I had to smile, sympathetically of course.

Figure 81 - Where the trail splits between Collegiate East and Collegiate West routes

The route I took treated me with a self-guided tour of the Interlaken Historic Site. It's a former resort dating back to the 1870s. At the time it was luxurious for a rustic mountain setting. Orchestras played in the summer and guests enjoyed sleigh rides in the winter. There were billiard tables made with rare woods and ivory inlays. It survived for a couple decades before the dam was built that turned the twin glacial lakes into a big reservoir with its shallow stagnant water, which contributed to the hotel's declining popularity. It went bust. The restoration began in 1972 by the US Bureau of Reclamation and the site is protected by its status as a National Register of Historic Places. (Inter-Laken Hotel 2018) It still attracts a good number of visitors during the summer months. I passed maybe 20 people along this trail heading to/from the site.

Figure 82 - Dexter's House at Interlaken

Figure 83 - Horse stables at Interlaken

From Interlaken I climbed another several miles, steep in some places, up Little Willis Gulch to an avalanche meadow to make camp. Along the way I met a couple from Ohio hiking the trail and later reconnected with Baine, who by now was hiking solo. The couple went further up the gulch to camp. Baine camped near me. We had a great talk, which was the start of a hiking partnership that would last for the next 75 miles.

The total mileage for the day was 19.3 with a little less than 3000 feet elevation gain. My feet were happy that I didn't break the newly established 20-mile rule.

> **Pro Tip:** I brought a set of night clothes (a merino wool long sleeve shirt, medium weight long underwear), and possumdown/merino wool socks that were only used at night. Dampness from clothes worn during the day would make for colder nights and tends to stink up the sleeping quilt/bag.

The next day I was up and on the trail before any of my compadres. The temp was near freezing. I could see frost on Baine's tent as I passed by. My tent was pitched under the cover of some pines, which helps reduce condensation and dew.

The Ohio couple camped near log cabin ruins up the trail about a mile.

Figure 84 - Several log cabin ruins along Little Willis Gulch

Figure 85 - One of the trail markers along Little Willis Gulch

The trail leading up to Hope Pass felt like a rite of passage. Many have spoken about this as the first tough pass, the "real" introduction to the Collegiate West, and the first of many spectacular views along the alternate route. It met expectation for its toughness. It did not disappoint with its views.

I was filled with wonder as I made my way to tree line, not a completely unfamiliar feeling to me since I had hiked above tree line dozens of times over the past several years. But this time it felt more intense. I walked through the opening space before me and stopped to admire the sun first drenching the mountains for the day. The shadows from the trees instructed my eyes to fix on Hope Mountain. Maybe it was a message that I should fix my hope on completing this mountain of a journey. It was one of those "be in the moment" moments, where my entire being was appreciating what I was experiencing. There were many of these kinds of moments along this trail.

Figure 86 - Breaking tree line on the way up Hope Pass

The top of the pass was gorgeous, giving me my first look at the expanse of the Collegiate West route. I could see several 14ers from here. This morning could not have been more perfect.

Figure 87 - the top of Hope Pass

Figure 88 - Kicking back on Hope Pass contemplating the route ahead

On my way down from Hope Pass I met a couple coming up. They were completing the Collegiate Loop; both were teachers from the Midwest spending part of their summer in these hills. Not a bad way to break from the classroom.

It wasn't long before the trail began to parallel County Road 390 near Winfield, where a few historic buildings still remain from the mining days. The trail doesn't pass by the buildings directly, but it's not much of a diversion.

There was some mountain lion scat on the trail. It keyed me to watch my surroundings. Big cats are elusive. To spot one is uncommon.

> **Pro Tip:** It is better to walk in groups when in mountain lion country. Being noisy will reduce the chances of surprising a lion. Other mountain lion safety tips: do not approach; give the lion a way to escape; talk calmly but firmly; move slowly; do not run; appear larger by raising arms or opening your jacket; don't turn your back to it; if the lion is aggressive, throw stones or anything you can get without crouching down. (Wildlife, Mountain Lions 2018)

Figure 89 - Turn off near Winfield - we're headed to Lake Ann Pass

Today was a low mileage day. Alternatively, I could have pushed further up toward or past Lake Ann Pass, but it wasn't in me to hike the additional elevation and miles today, and I wanted a warmer night by sleeping lower. There was no rush.

I set my mind on getting into the Collegiate Wilderness Area, getting to the 200-mile marker, and camping along the South Fork of Clear Creek. I would take on Lake Ann Pass the next morning.

Figure 90 - Entering the Collegiate Wilderness Area

Shortly after entering the Collegiate Wilderness Area I came across a father-son pair resting among some pines. We talked a while about my journey but I was more interested in their journey. The son was living in California. He looked to be college age. The father was from near Boston. They were a broken family on the mend, taking this time to reconnect. There is no better place than nature to mend brokenness and neither of them was in a hurry for this experience to end.

A mile or so later I came across a father-daughter pair who were day hiking Lake Ann Pass. The daughter was maybe an early teenager. Both were physically fit and had spent a fair amount of time in these mountains. It was obvious the connection between them was strong. We had a nice conversation about the day, the trail, and how magical this place was.

How great is it to see families together out here, or anywhere, thoroughly enjoying themselves? To me it's one of the things that affirms my belief that spending time in the wilderness is powerful and special, that this kind of activity in these places somehow aligns us with how and what we're supposed to be: happy, fulfilled, and completed.

Up ahead around a couple more bends in the trail it opened up to an amazing view of the Apostle Peaks and Ice Mountain. It literally made me stop in my tracks and stare. I found a rock to sit on for a while and just soaked it in.

There were many views like this along the trail, but something special about this setting was all consuming. In my next breath I spoke to God with a word of thanks, not just for what I was seeing and experiencing, but for everything I've been given. There are times when the trail becomes a spiritual experience, when we are overwhelmed, when we have an emotional reaction to the sum of our surroundings, when we are humbled by the enormity of what our senses are taking in, when we are suddenly so incredibly small and overcome by an intense gratefulness for existing. This was one of those experiences for me. And I'm not sure I would have had it if I were not alone at the moment. Solitude has a way of giving us permission to open wide and to be vulnerable, soul sensitive.

Figure 91 - The Apostle Peaks and Ice Mountain

Figure 92 - 200 miles on the trail!

This day marked 200 miles on the trail. I finished the first segment of the Collegiate West Route (CW01) and hiked 7.1 miles into CW02. It was 11.4 miles and 2000 feet elevation gain. I was OK with the short day.

> **Pro Tip:** Toss the sleeping bag (or top quilt) stuff sack. I put an industrial trash bag in my pack as a waterproof liner, and the first thing I put in is my

quilt. The stuff sack creates wasted space around it. By putting my quilt in without a stuff sack, it just gets squashed at the bottom creating less wasted space. Do the same with your sleeping pad and air pillow if you can. The trash bag protects everything in my pack from getting wet.

The next day was August 1st. I was now two weeks on the trail. It started with a climb past Lake Ann and up to Lake Ann Pass. Everyone should start their day with a view like this.

I passed the Ohio couple still in their tent. Baine had made it to Lake Ann and cowboy camped next to the lake with another hiker he had met up there. I would meet up with Baine later.

Figure 93 - Lake Ann

Figure 94 - The trail to Lake Ann Pass

Up the trail to Lake Ann Pass I could see that some of the cornice from the past winter had not yet completely melted. I had read about this cornice and the difficulty maneuvering around it earlier in the season. I imagined the winter winds howling through the pass to create such a lasting mark of the season.

About this time, I recalled the weekend I had climbed Huron Peak a few years ago. While I was in camp the night before a few young ragged men walked by. They had just returned from their attempt to find Lake Ann, wondering around these rugged mountains in early June with the snow still heavy above tree line. They must have been post-holing up there in the snow, grooming their own trail for hours. They were unsuccessful at finding Lake Ann. One of the guys had blown out his shoe. It was in tatters and held together by duct tape. They were heading to Buena Vista so he could get a new pair.

I remember thinking how young and adventurous they were. I was a little envious, both about their age and sense of adventure. I also thought about how crazy they were to be up here without adequate navigational skills, yet they found their way back. Tough and fearless, and maybe foolish, they were. But

I suppose that's the definition of an adventurous spirit.

Zoom ahead a few years. Here I am, just a few miles from where I saw those young adventurers. I'm not in the same tough conditions, but I am convincingly older, and I am on a 500-mile trek through the same mountains. The envy is diminishing. I'm feeling strong and confident. It's my turn, my way.

Figure 95 - Half way up Lake Ann Pass - Huron Peak pointing up in the center

Figure 96 - The top of Lake Ann Pass

The other side of the pass was less spectacular, but not without its own beauty, and still begged my curiosity. What will come my way next?

Figure 97 - Looking down the south side of Lake Ann Pass

Figure 98 - More plush forests

On the way down the Pass I spoke with an older lady (I

would guess in her 70s) who was about to finish the Collegiate Loop in a couple days. Wow! Go, girl! I did warn her about the scree and loose talus on the other side. I felt nervous for her but knew that if she made it this far that there was no obstacle up ahead that she couldn't handle. She'd be fine. What an inspiration! (I didn't get her picture or name)

Figure 99 - Looking toward Texas Creek/Waterloo Gulch

Nearly 10 miles in as I was filtering water from Texas Creek I was thinking that I had not seen the couple from Ohio or Baine yet today. Then guess who shows up? Baine! He had taken a wrong turn down the western slope and ended up adding 3 miles and 1500 feet elevation to his day. He wasn't thrilled about that move. We agreed to go on together as far as we could.

> **Pro Tip:** Everyone takes a wrong turn. When you do, don't panic. Sit for a minute, look at your GPS or map to get your bearings. Backtrack on the same trail until you get to the intersection where you made a wrong turn, no matter how far. Don't try fancy short-cuts or bushwhacking; the terrain can get nasty fast. Stay calm; there's no hurry.

We ended up making camp a couple miles short of Cottonwood Pass at an unnamed pond next to the trail. The Ohio couple showed up a little while later, making their camp on the opposite side of the pond.

As the sun was setting we fixed dinner on some logs by a fire pit. We didn't make a fire as we weren't sure if the fire ban had been lifted. By then it was starting to get dark.

Along the way we couldn't help but notice the beetle kill devastation in some portions of these forests. Many pine trees are left standing dead. I have a URSack; it's a bear proof food sack that can be tied around the base of a small tree or on any limb that will support it. It's not a big chore. Other people don't have bear proof bags. They face the challenge of having to hang their bag on extended limbs 15 feet above the ground (ideally). Pine trees are not ideal for bear bag hanging; it can be a challenge. Care should be taken on these beetle kill trees because, as in the case tonight, Baine had a tree fall dangerously close to him while trying to hang his food in it. It was a mighty crash. Baine's OK; I laughed; I couldn't help myself. So, the next time you hear a falling tree in the woods, check to see if your hiking partner is OK.

A little about the Mountain Pine Beetle: They are small and black about the size of a grain of rice. They survive on extracting nutrients from under the bark of several different varieties of pine (ponderosa, whitebark, lodgepole, scotch, and jack pine) and are normally good for the forest. As the nutrients diminish, the tree dies and usually quickly. The normal behavior for the beetle is to only attack old and weakened trees, allowing for the development of a younger, healthier forest. It's a grand design, balancing the natural life cycle of the forest. But when things are out of balance beetle activity can flourish and cause a more severe impact on the forest. In Colorado from 1996-2017 the impact was 3.4 million acres, the greatest was in 2008. (C. S. Service 2018) That's about the size of Connecticut. There are many factors that lead to this imbalance. Among them are forest fire suppression efforts which increase food sources for the insect, cycles of warmer summers and mild winters which increase the time of impact, and various attempts over decades to control beetle populations which further disrupt the natural cycles, habitats, and behaviors. (Barker 2003) (Canada 2018) (Florida 2018) The short story here is that it's complicated, but these little critters can be quite impactful.

Back to the hike... this day's totals were 4000 feet elevation gain and 16.3 miles. We're still in CW02.

Tomorrow will be a long day if we do the entire CW03 – which we should, because we'll be above tree line all day and our camping and exit options are limited and inconvenient. We'll see what the day brings.

Figure 100 - Camp at the pond a couple miles short of Cottonwood Pass

Figure 101 - The pond near Cottonwood Pass

The first goal the next morning was to get up and over Cottonwood Pass. This will complete CW02. The Ohio couple were first out of camp. Baine and I followed shortly after. The early morning sun made for a misty blue morning of rolling mountain tops in the western Sawatch Mountain Range. As much as we needed to move on, the views earned our pause and admiration.

Figure 102 - The approach to Cottonwood Pass

Figure 103 - The final approach to Cottonwood Pass

Figure 104 - Yours truly on top of Cottonwood Pass

We took a short break on top of the Pass before crossing over to fill our water at the small pond. The Sawatch and Elk Ranges were stunning. The Pass was closed to vehicle traffic because they were widening and paving the road on west side of the Pass. It is expected to be closed to vehicle traffic until the spring of 2019.

Figure 105 - The Elk Range, looking west from Cottonwood Pass

CW03, for anyone familiar with the Sawatch Range, goes essentially from Mount Harvard to Mount Princeton. I had climbed all the Collegiate Peaks in my peak bagging days a few years back. Seeing these mountains from the opposite side was a first for me. I was a little surprised at how well I recognized the features of each of these big peaks from this side of the range.

Remembering back to when I was leaving the Interlaken site, I met up with a couple guys who had just finished the Collegiate West. They talked about the change in temperature, winds, and challenges of the hike. But they described it all as well worth the investment. I was about to find out.

Immediately after Cottonwood Pass the trail rose to what became the first of several climbs for the day. The trail would rise and fall between saddles, tributaries, ridges, and streams. The highest point is around 12,800 feet and lowest point is around 11,000 feet at the end of CW03 at Tincup Pass Road.

What follows is a series of pictures from CW03.

Figure 106 - The trail after the first ascent past Cottonwood Pass

Figure 107 - Baine as we head into CW03

Figure 108 - Some unnamed water features. County Road 306 is in the valley left, Jones Mountain North is prominent center-right.

Figure 109 - I hate to break it to you, Lost Lake is now found

Figure 110 - Jones Mountain on our left as the trail heads down toward Mineral Basin

Figure 111 - A few alpine flowers holding on

Figure 112 - One of the few water sources on CW03 - using a leaf as a funnel

Figure 113 - Rough terrain below Emma Burr Mountain

Figure 114 - Skies are starting to darken as we approach our descent to Tincup Pass Road

"Dream with me" became the theme of the day as we wound our way through the high terrain, up high and then low, through talus and scree, through one breathtaking view after another. Dream about a great water source. Dream about where the trail is actually taking us. Dream about the weather cooperating. Dream about less talus. But more importantly, pinch yourself, because this beautiful place is like walking in an awesome dream.

> **Pro Tip:** Taking **The Colorado Trail Databook** is definitely a valuable asset on the trail. I separated my Databook, only carrying the pages I needed between resupply points. I bound the pages together with a small carabiner through a hole I punched in the corner. It reduced the weight from 7.4oz to 1.5oz.

I broke off the end of one of my trekking poles in the talus. It's a common mishap as it's easy to lodge the tips of these poles between the rocks. Without realizing it, as you move forward the pole doesn't come with you. Something has to give; sometimes it's the pole.

The Ohio couple were with us for a while but dropped back after about 5 miles. They were contemplating getting below tree line as the weather didn't look favorable to them. We didn't see them afterward. It didn't rain until 9pm when we had only a slow drizzle for a short time. But the weather is difficult to accurately predict up here. Spending more time above tree line in questionable conditions is always a risk.

Near Jones Mountain we had filtered some water at a small stream. It was here we first met Rabbit and a few of his newly formed trail friends. I connected up with them a few more times further down the trail.

We made camp near Tincup Pass Road, a stone's throw from the North Fork of Chalk Creek. The trail down to the road was steep with many switchbacks. We had put in 18.4 miles with an elevation gain of around 4000 feet. It took us just under 12 hours.

Rabbit and friends had camped a little further down from us, just a few feet from the creek. We saw them packing up on our way out in the morning. They told us about a moose they had seen in the area.

The day started with crossing the North Fork of Chalk Creek and climbing 1200 feet to a pass. The landscape was slowly changing once again into a subalpine region.

Figure 115 - Looking back as we climbed our first pass of the day

Coming down off the pass we made our way to Tunnel Gulch where we followed an abandon narrow gage railroad grade. Some of the old railroad ties were still in place. It was abandon in 1910.

Figure 116 - Old narrow gauge railroad grade

It was raining off and on from late morning to mid-afternoon. Rabbit and crew passed us at one of our water stops but we would later catch up with them sheltered in some pines from the rain. I was entertaining some questions about my rain gear - The Packa. It's one garment that is a pack cover, rain jacket, and parka all in one. It works great for hiking, but if you need to stop to take off your pack in the rain you will get wet because the jacket comes off with the pack.

Rabbit has taken like wildfire to this thru-hiking life. When asked if he had plans to do more thru-hiking, he didn't pause a second. I can't wait to hear about his future adventures.

Figure 117 – Rabbit (picture provided by Rabbit)

Soon we were at Hancock Trailhead and followed a 4x4

road to Hancock Lakes, both above tree line. A few brave fishermen were trying their skills against the wind and rain. Diehards they are. As for me, I'm just following this path.

Figure 118 - Hancock Lakes

We climbed up another pass and descended to a view of Mount Aetna. Then it was on to the end of CW04 at Boss Lake Trailhead. There was plenty of water in this section. We crossed some rock slide areas and eventually climbed up to Boss Lake. It was more intense than expected, ending at the dam. It was here we finally had cell service so we called family and friends. After talking with Bobbi, I called Pagosa and Kristie to coordinate the resupply at CO114 in 4 days.

Figure 119 - Periodic rock slide areas

Figure 120 - Butterflies Grazing

Figure 121 - Standing on the Dam at Boss Lake

We made camp at Hunt Lake a couple miles up the trail from Boss Lake. It's starting to get chilly. I needed to dawn the puffy.

Figure 122 - Hunt Lake

We finished CW04 (15.9 miles) and hiked 2.3 miles into CW05 for a total of 18.2 miles with 3700 feet elevation gain. We are now in the last segment of the Collegiate West route – CW05. It's a little sad to be leaving this, but excited to experience what is to come.

A line out of the Guthooks app described our next water source as "sweet as angelic baby spit". It made us laugh. It was a half mile up the trail from camp. Being out of camp at 7:30 put us at this magical water source within minutes.

Figure 123 - The source of angelic baby spit

The Continental Divide was just a short way up from here. We soon gained the Divide and enjoyed another crazy beautiful 360 view. There was still some climbing to do, but most of the trail was flat or down to Monarch Pass.

Figure 124 - Up on the Continental Divide again

The terrain from here begins to mellow as we headed toward Monarch Pass. One interesting historical site along the way was ruins of old game herding rock walls, where native tribes would steer herds of elk and deer into entrapments. Some of the structures were still faintly visible. A plaque at the site tells the story.

Figure 125 - The trail toward Monarch Pass

Figure 126 - Monarch Ski Area straight ahead

The trail led us through Monarch Ski Mountain and then down to the Monarch Pass Gift Shop. Cheese nachos and hand scooped ice cream were had. I also recharged my Anker battery source... which took hours... and picked up my resupply box.

The two hikers who had missed their turn onto the Collegiate East route back near Twin Lakes came in while I was there. It was good catching up with them. Rabbit came in briefly and then headed down to Salida with his other hiking partners. I also talked with a guy from Texas who was quite introspective and touched by the trail.

The gift shop had a well-stocked hiker box. A hiker box contains usable food or gear items hikers leave behind. It's usually items that a person no longer wants to carry or maybe it's food the hiker has come to dislike. The items are free for the taking.

The folks who own the shop are good and accommodating people. But one quirky thing is that they don't want hikers walking around with their packs. Instead, they have a hiker corner where we can store our packs, go through the hiker box, recharge batteries, pack up our resupply, or just hang out on the floor (there's no furniture).

I said my good bye to Baine at the Pass. His mother was his

ride to some family time and then back to medical school. He's a curious and intelligent man with a great appetite for living full. Someday I'll know a famous guy who changed the world; it'll be Baine. He made for a fun hiking partner who tolerated my sense of humor and speed. He kept saying I was keeping up with him (he's 25 years younger), but we both know if he turned it on he would have been much further ahead. We exchanged contact information, as we were both grateful for our time on the trail together and vowed to keep in touch.

> **Pro Tip:** Battery conservation can be critical, especially in emergency situations. Be sure to ration battery usage on emergency electronic devices in a way that will ensure plenty of battery life. You'll need it should you become stranded for a day or two. My **Anker PowerCore 10000** was used to recharge my phone and GPS unit.

I'll be solo again until I meet up with another compatible hiker. I like this cadence. Sometimes I'm hiking with someone, and I've also had my alone time. Both are good for me.

After my batteries were nearly charged (I didn't feel like waiting hours longer for the full charge), I hiked up another few miles and set up camp at the base of a ridge near a cluster of pines. Only 15 minutes later more storms rolled over me... rain, pea size hail, thunder, wind. I was so thankful I decided not to press ahead!!

Sadly, the Collegiate West route is coming to a close. It was glorious, tough, rewarding, and had some of the best scenery on the tail. I met some people here that I suspect I will be in touch with for years to come. These kind of places inspire these kinds of relationships.

Figure 127 - The storms roll in and out

CHAPTER SEVEN

Out of the Collegiate West to
Cochetopa Creek Headwaters

T he off-and-on stormy weather from the night before on the ridge just a few miles south of Monarch Pass continued throughout the next day. I had prayed to be safely below tree line before the first storm and the request was honored.

Since the trail gives us time to think, I began to wonder about prayers for weather. One would think that the complexity of global weather patterns and the sure need for some sort of atmospheric balancing act would make for some difficulty in granting such a request. It's not a small ask. The assumption I was making is that if my day was favorable it would need to be unfavorable somewhere else, perhaps on someone else. Whose day am I ruining by making my day better? It all somehow seemed quite selfish to request good weather for myself. And what if there are other similar requests for the same, maybe thousands around the world. I hope I didn't cause a mess. In any case, I was safe from bad weather today.

The views and scenery today, compared to my previous few days are far less dramatic for sure, but that didn't mean less beauty.

Figure 128 - Early morning, blue skies - for a little while

From my camp I was only a few miles short of ending CW05 and reconnecting with Segment 15. I most certainly will miss the Collegiate West. But it's time to celebrate. The Collegiate West is complete! It was the part of the trail that presented itself to me as the crux of the journey. And I did it!

This place marking the end of CW05 was empowering, probably the most defining point on the trail for me. It was here that I first truly envisioned that I would finish this trail. I stepped forward from this place with a new confidence, an empowered bounce in my step.

Figure 129 - A marker at the end of CW05

For those who might be accustomed to shelters along the trail, like the Appalachian Trail, the CT has one, only one shelter. It's the Green Creek Shelter a couple miles from the CW05/ Segment 15 intersection.

Figure 130 - The only shelter on the CT - The Green Creek Shelter

Note: As evidenced by the above picture, it was right about here that the memory card in my camera became corrupt. I didn't realize it had gone bad until much further down the trail. And so, the pictures for the next few Segments will be only ones I took from my phone.

This day was also a day of losing things. I couldn't find my tooth brush and lip balm when I was breaking camp in the morning. Fortunately, I found them later as I was setting up camp. I had stuffed them in a place I wouldn't normally put them.

I also lost one of my sun gloves, the pair given to me by Pagosa. I did not find it again. I'm sure I left it at the creek where I took a break early in the day to wash myself and my socks. In my haste to get my Packa on as it started raining again I must have dropped it or left it by the creek. Little things like this can make for a frustrating day, even if the rest of the day was otherwise fantastic.

I got my first blister too, on the side of one of my toes. I didn't notice until it came time to clean my feet before bed. I dressed it up. Not bad – only one blister and I'm over halfway through the hike.

I saw some bikers riding in the thunder and lightning. I later asked another set of bikers about standard behavior and precautions for bikers in that type of weather. They don't ride in lightning. In fact, one of them told me he separates himself from his bike by at least 50 feet during a lightning storm. His answer was more in line with what I thought might be the more reasonable approach to biker safety on the trail.

Pro Tip: Joe Lindsey, a 25-year veteran of adventure biking, writes about his experience in a lightning storm on the CT very near to where I was on this day. His advice is to seek shelter, avoid grouping together, cover to stay dry, and descend to safer terrain. (Lindsey 2017)

After 100 miles without a shower I have come to realize

that a person may not be suited for thru-hiking if cleanliness is a serious priority. I met Talus again yesterday at the Monarch Pass Gift Shop. He was looking hobo dirty. (He admitted as much) I saw several hikers today who were especially ragged looking. Then I considered myself and how unkept I appeared in the mirror yesterday at Monarch Pass. And that I decided to carry deodorant and make it a priority to clean up every day probably puts me on the outer fringe of the thru-hiking culture. It's not that thru-hikers like to be dirty; it's just that when they are, it's OK; it's almost expected; it's part of the deal.

Several people have told me that I don't look like a thru-hiker because I look (relatively) clean and my BO is less assaulting than they expected. I'm not exactly sure if those comments were meant to be compliments or some statement of doubt. But I've chosen to be complimented, because what I'm hearing is "gee, you're not as much of a dirtbag as I was expecting".

I made it past Marshall Pass today, the end of Segment 15. My camp was 4 miles into Segment 16 at the intersection of Silver Creek Trail. After setting up my tent and hanging my Packa out to dry, a few hikers came by and sat for a few minutes. They broke out a jar of peanut butter and tortillas, Snickers, and trail bars. This is the sustenance formula of many on the trail. Several groups of bikers peddled by as we made small talk. Soon they were nourished enough to move on and I was ready to cook up my dinner with a great sunset view of Mount KIA/MIA and Sheep Mountain Northeast, a rewarding finish to my day.

The next day, August 6th, was a very productive day. I put in 18 miles and 3500 feet elevation gain through some of the worst trail conditions so far in the CT. There was lots of loose rock and the trail torn up by motorbikes. Mostly I felt today was just a necessary means to an end. There are spectacular trail days and there are those that bring you closer to the next spectacular trail day. This was one of those. Although, it did have some highlights.

I saw what appeared to be fresh moose tracks on the trail not long after I started. A cow moose, it turns out, was just minutes ahead of me. I caught up with her as she muscled her way up a small embankment, not 20 feet from me when I saw her. I stopped in my tracks. I recalled a dangerous moose encounter I had a few years back while hiking in the Buffalo Peaks Wilderness Area outside of Buena Vista. It was a young bull that nearly ran me over in what was later described to me as a false charge. They are big, powerful animals that don't always fear humans.

I backed up a bit as she hid herself behind a spruce tree. Not knowing what she would do next and not knowing if one of her calves was nearby, I was thinking she might feel compelled to defend the territory or her offspring.

As I slowly walked forward again, confident that no young ones were near, I saw that she had moved a relatively safe distance from the trail. I say "relatively safe" because moose can run up to 30 miles per hour, which wouldn't have given me much time to consider my options had she decided to come my way. I felt comfortable enough to move on, looking behind me every few steps. She sounded a couple snorts and that was the last I saw or heard from her.

> **Pro Tip:** Moose are not interested in eating you, but they can be dangerous. Moose can charge people if they are stressed, cornered, being harassed (by people or dogs), during mating season in September and October, or during calving season in late spring. Look for raised hackles along its shoulders, pinned back ears, or lowered head. If you see any of these or if it starts moving toward you, move away and seek cover as soon as possible. Maintain a safe distance and know that you can't outrun a moose. (Maloney 2017)

This is also a good time to remind folks that these trails aren't just for humans. All kinds of critters find these trails convenient. I cringe when I see people camping on or very near trails, knowing that it's just a matter of time before they'll have an uninvited guest enter their personal space.

I also saw 5 deer, all young, three buck and two does. Bucks still have their velvet this time of year.

A couple families of grouse were also along the trail today not far from where I spotted a fox.

The wildlife was plentifully today, which might have been because I was traveling alone and relatively quiet as compared to hiking with a group of people.

Sargents Mesa was the highlight of the day. One disappointment was that I unknowingly passed the connecting trail that would have allowed me to view the memorial to Indochina veterans near the high point of the mesa. It's a place called Soldierstone. It's an odd place for a memorial as there are no roads to it; a fence has been put up some distance from the site to keep motorbikes from ruining the fragile terrain; it's in quite an isolated spot, unusual and unique.

A veteran by the name of Stuart Allen Beckley built it. Beckley is a retired U.S. Army Lieutenant Colonel who served in the Vietnam War. The intent of the memorial was to offer a tribute from American soldiers to the forgotten soldiers from "Vietnam, Laos, Cambodia, the Hmong, the Montagnard Tribes of Central Vietnam, the Koreans, Thais, French, Germans, Slavs, North Africans, Black Africans, and others who were ... expended... for the people of Indochina, [from] 1945 through 1975."

Mike Donelson, owner of Ark Valley Memorial, in Rocky Ford, Colorado custom built the memorial for Beckley without charging him for his time or labor.

Beckley scouted the CT along the Continental Divide for a National Forest site. In 1995 after much pleading with the U.S. Forest Service he was granted permission to put the memorial in its current place. He also demanded no publicity, no open congressional hearings, and no media. It was to be an anonymous American soldiers' tribute to those forgotten soldiers.

Soldierstone was erected in July of 1995. Beckley died on November 5th, 1995 and because of illness he never went to the

site. (Hood 2014)

In honoring the wishes of Colonel Beckley, I don't point out the exact location of the memorial. But know that this is a special place with solemn meaning.

I walked alone on my way up the ascent with plenty of time to think, heavy pack from a fresh load of water, as this area does not have many water sources. It reminded me of the loneliness and toil combat veterans endured. My brother-in-law paid his life in Vietnam. My uncle served during the Korean conflict and mostly kept it to himself all his life. And many others from many countries gave all for the sake of Indochina peoples. The walk was emotional for me; it was personal. So, even if I didn't see the memorial, I felt that I paid my respects on the trail. The service of these men and women, especially those who gave all, is beyond what a grateful nation can repay. We are forever indebted.

Figure 131 - The path leading up to Sargents Mesa

Figure 132 - Sargents Mesa and the end of Segment 16

I did not meet any southbound hikers today. I did meet up with one CT biker. We had a nice but brief conversation. The motorbikers, however, were not in the mood for conversation. Going unreasonably fast and ripping up the trail seemed to be their thing.

I noticed the abundance of flowers in the forest among the beetle-kill. The now sun-lit forest allows for a wide array of flowers on the forest floor. There can be beauty in disaster.

I finished Segment 16 and hiked 6.9 miles into Segment 17, camping where the CT intersects with the trail down to Baldy Lake. I thought about camping down by the lake, but up higher means less condensation in the tent, plus I didn't want to add 400 more feet of elevation gain the next day.

After the sun had set several groups of bikers rode by camp. Some people like to night hike/bike. I didn't do any of that on this trip. I think I'm less interested in big miles that night hiking would get me. I'm more interested in seeing all the sights of the trail.

The next day was another milestone day. I passed the 300-mile point! In the beginning of the hike, 500 miles seems so far off, almost unachievable. And now that I'm over half way it definitely seems within reach.

Figure 133 - 300 miles achieved!

I guess I don't think about that 500-mile number anymore. I think about what I need to do today, one day at a time. I am learning more how to live for the day and in the moment. I suppose that's not unlike how a person goes about achieving any large goal: one step, one small achievement at a time.

There was much elevation loss today. I don't always talk about elevation loss because it seems like less of an achievement. But, downhill isn't easy. Longer stretches or steep periods of downhill can take a toll on the knees and quads. But, it does make for bigger and faster mileage.

> **Pro Tip:** Use the heel lock lacing technique to prevent jamming toes and possibly (eventually) loosing toe nails when hiking downhill. Start by kicking you're your heel so your feet go to the back of your shoe, then while your heel is still kicked back, loosen the lower lacing just a little and use a double overhand knot near the top to help lock the laces in place so they don't slip or loosen. Then at the top use crossover lacing for higher boots or for lower boots tie the top a little tighter than normal to make sure it's nice and snug. A video demo is on the Appalachian Mountain Club site or other places online. (Heid 2013)

Kristie and a friend met me at the intersection of CO114 this afternoon to drop off my resupply. While we were talking, 4 thru-bikers rode by. Kristy asked them if they wanted some of the drinks and food she brought along, which was a generous supply. So, they joined us and we talked for quite some time.

One of the bikers was a grief counselor at Columbine High on April 20, 1999 at the time of the school shootings. He runs a non-profit now in New Mexico, inspired by his experience at Columbine. This bike trip was a memorial ride for him. I could tell for him it was still emotionally fresh.

I swapped out my shoes. The Altra Timps are comfortable when they are new, but after a few hundred miles they seem to have lost cushioning and tread.

Thanks again to Kristie, I'm all resupplied and I'm carrying a day and a half of water, since I'll have no reliable water source for the next 20 miles. The pack is heavy.

Tonight I slept at just about 10k feet. It's been a while since I've slept this low. I can feel it in the air too. It's not as crisp tonight. I finished Segment 17 and hiked 3.3 miles into Segment 18 for a total of 17 miles and 2200 feet elevation gain. Good day.

The terrain where I found a flat enough camp site was challenging because for several miles it was sloping ground on both sides of the trail and for as far as I could see into the woods. But after I set up camp I wondered around a bit only to find a very nice place with a fire pit that was a hundred feet further off trail next to a bluff with a nice view. I was too tired to move my tent. I remember the soil there was like powder and it was incredibly dry. One young lady passed by while I was setting up. She ended up camping literally on the trail a few hundred feet up. And lucky for her, no critters bothered her that night.

The next day was an even bigger day. I had a heavy pack and I needed to put in some miles through high, dry, and hot terrain to get to the next reliable water source.

I entered cattle country. As I walked through the barren land filled with sagebrush and other drought tolerant plant life, I imagined the early cattle drives, cowboys crossing the land. It has its own beauty and cannot be fully appreciated without the hot sun and dry wind. There was nearly 20 miles of this experience today. I feel like I could not have appreciated it more. I'm was full.

Figure 134 - Hot, dry cattle country

I met a half dozen thru-hikers today. One of them was desperately low on water seven miles from any water source. I gave her a liter of my supply, even while her and her hiking partner were unashamedly ridiculing hikers who carried more than they should.

Well, I didn't feel bad for carrying the extra weight and I did feel good about helping a fellow hiker. So, for anyone who writes books on thru-hiking, please include a few words on topics other than those who can move faster and carry less weight. Because once in a while that heavier, slower hiker carrying the extra water will be the trail angle that less prepared, but lighter, hiker will appreciate.

I was elated to reach Cochetopa Creek, that is until I saw dozens of cows walking and defecating in the creek, the same creek from which I had been dreaming of filtering cold, clean water. I wasn't overly concerned because I had brought a very good water purification system, but just the thought of getting drinking water out of a cattle septic system was unappealing. I filtered my water a little upstream where it "looked" cleaner. I had done the same thing earlier along the trail.

Other hikers I had joined were filtering using less efficient systems. They were not pleased with the taste of the water, even after adding flavored powder. But, it's part of this thru-hiking world. If the filter keeps out stuff that will cause sickness, even if it doesn't taste good, it's good enough.

Pro Tip: Water filtration/purification is usually a topic of discussion compounded by misinformation. The simple fact is that only one method is effective at removing all pathogens from backcountry water: boiling. All other methods are lacking. Since none of the human senses can detect the presence of Cryptosporidium, Giardia, bacteria (such as campylobacter, salmonella, etc.) or viruses (such as enterovirus, hepatitis A, norovirus, etc.), it is important to take precautions. My only advice is to understand the facts and then make an informed and calculated decision about which treatment method will work for you. The consequences of a bad decision can be extremely uncomfortable... or worse. The CDC put out a fact sheet on backcountry water treatment. (CDC 2009) I used an **MSR Guardian** Water Purifier, which filters down to .02 microns – it will filter all bacteria and many viruses. The popular **Sawyer Squeeze** filters filter down to .1 microns – it's less effective (but maybe effective enough for the CO backcountry) but a pound lighter.

The last few miles I followed Cochetopa Creek up stream to where the trail crosses the creek. My tent set up was about 50 feet above the creek. The first task tomorrow is to forge across it; the bridge is washed out.

I had put in a little over 20 miles today and around 2200 feet elevation gain, finishing Segment 18 and hiking 9.7 miles of Segment 19. Yes, the feet rebelled. Deep blisters were forming on the outside of both heels. They were a bit painful. I treated them the best I could, but I may visit a medic in Lake City if I don't see progress.

The next morning my first few steps on the trail were barefoot across Cochetopa Creek. It was the only true forge of the trail so far. And it was the perfect thing for a morning without caffeine; a cold stomp through an ice cold creek is a good wake-me-up. Breakfast was above the creek on a nice grassy shelf, just after sunrise. It felt really nice to warm my feet in the sun.

Most of who I met yesterday are long gone ahead of me. That is except for a mother-daughter couple. The mother's trail name is Soulshine and daughter goes by Mariposa, which happens to be the model name of my backpack – Spanish for "butterfly". We passed each other off and on throughout the day before as we would today.

The trail today essentially followed the creek to its headwaters as it rose above tree line to 11,755 feet. This is where I set up camp among the willow bushes.

Figure 135 - Hiking up Cochetopa Creek.

When I arrived at camp I met a family who had been hiking the area all day; a mother and father with two children. They asked me why I was on the trail. I told them vaguely that it was a good timing for me with regard to my health. She revealed that she had a life threatening illness a few years back. She talked about the time she had remaining with her family was going to be spent with great intention. She had vowed to live the rest of her days being as alive as she could be. What a breath of fresh air she was! We could have talked more, but the sky was getting nasty again, so they took off for lower ground. The sky opened up minutes later.

Shortly after the storm Soulshine and Mariposa came walking into camp. We all talked a bit before they decided to head up the trail even further. Their intent was to camp up high and hike San Luis Peak for a sunrise summit. The peak is one of Colorado's 14ers. It would be chilly but they won't forget the experience.

Figure 136 - Mariposa (left) and Soulshine (picture provided by Soulshine) taken later down the trail

Several others decided to camp near me. There was Ken from Fort Collins in Colorado, his son, Joe from Pennsylvania, and High-5. It was a welcome situation for me, having camped alone since Monarch Pass. We had dinner together and talked about the trail and what lead them all here. I'm sure we'll get to know each other more tomorrow.

Segment 19 is behind me. Camp is at 7.6 miles into Segment 20. This made the totals for today at 11.6 miles and 2000 feet elevation gain – an easy trail day.

CHAPTER EIGHT

*Cochetopa Creek Headwaters
to Elk Creek Headwaters*

Leaving camp at the headwaters of Cochetopa Creek started off with a cool breeze, but clear skies. Ken, his son, and Joe left camp about a half hour after I did. High-5 left before me. We were all headed up 2500 feet to summit San Luis Peak. It was a diversion of 3 miles out-and-back and 1500 feet elevation gain from the CT. It would be the 30th 14er I've summited.

The first big decision of the day was whether to carry our packs up to the summit or not. High-5 and I had arrived at the saddle first and decided I would set up my tent and put our packs in the tent. This was to keep the rodents (pica and marmot) from getting into our packs.

The climb went well. The trail had some loose rock, like most 14ers, but it was mostly a nontechnical straight shot with a couple false summits. And the views were great.

Figure 137 – A view from the summit of San Luis Peak

On my way down I met Ken, his son, and Joe climbing up. Joe was lagging behind – the expected flatlander behavior - but he was doing great so far in Colorado. When we were on the summit at 9am I noticed clouds were building already, a sign of another stormy afternoon ahead. I was concerned, with the high terrain ahead of us that they might not make their planned destination today. Ken had figured 10 miles should be the minimum goal for the day. But I know they would be smart about the weather, staying away from alpine areas during thunderstorms. I did not see them again after this encounter.

My plan was to finish Segment 20 and get at least a few miles into the next Segment. This meant that after the San Luis summit I had a 500-foot, 1000-foot, and another 500-foot climb, descending between each. All these climbs were above tree line, making the weather a significant consideration.

> **Pro Tip:** Lightning is no joke above tree line. But really, no place is safe from lightning outdoors. The safest places are in a forest or in a gully that's in a forest. The National Weather Service has a very informative brochure on the subject: **https:// www.weather.gov/media/safety/**

backcountry_lightning.pdf

Well, the storms moved in as expected. Half way up the 1000 foot climb it was thundering all around me. The rain started to fall and I was exposed. So I could either go back, losing the altitude I gained; sit in the rain until it passed; or set up my tent and hide out in there. I set up my tent. By then I had been hiking with Michael, an Aussie from Sydney. I believe this was my first international encounter on the trail. He chose to descend, probably thinking my plan was outside of his risk tolerance.

The rain stopped, Michael hiked back up to me, and we both decided to make a run for it before it turned bad again. The weather turned in our favor for that climb. Michael took a break; I moved on.

Near the end of the final 500-foot climb the thunder started again. I was one mile from where I wanted to set up camp so I gave it my all. By this time, I had caught up with Soulshine and Mariposa. We exchanged a few words. I asked them about their San Luis sunrise experience, which they were still gleaming about. They mentioned that they had noticed me behind them some time ago and how they thought I had been pacing hard as it wasn't long before I caught up. I didn't think my pace was any faster, but maybe I was motivated to get away from the weather. They stayed a bit to take a little rest. This was the last time I would see them. I moved on. Once again I was racing with the weather to set up camp. And once again I got the tent set up just in time.

Camp was close but slightly above Middle Mineral Creek. I had crossed into La Garita Wilderness Area a few miles before camp.

The rain continued quite a while, hard at times. I set up my mattress and laid back enjoying the sound of the rain on the tent, a smile on my face. It was a great day. I was thankful for it.

When the rain stopped I got out of my tent just in time to be startled by a series of loud splashes. A cow moose had been spooked by a hiker coming the opposite direction down the trail. She ran into a nearby beaver pond. I talked with the hiker; he seemed oblivious to how dangerous these horse-size creatures can be. I didn't press it but hoped my reaction to his cavalier attitude toward the beast might cause him to reexamine his lack of respect.

Shortly after the moose experience I had my dinner and turned in for the night. I heard a small group of people setting up camp not far from me. I didn't get out of my tent to see; I was too comfortable and not curious enough to see who it was. The next day I discovered it was Rabbit and friends. I would meet up with them again the next morning a few miles down the trail on Snow Mesa.

Today I finished Segment 20 and hiked 3.9 miles into Segment 21, plus summited San Luis Peak. Totals for the day: 12 miles and 4500 feet elevation gain. Today was the highest gain so far on this hike.

I woke early (5am) the next day with a thin layer of ice inside and outside my tent. Chilly night, for sure. But I had on enough layers to keep me warm.

There was a bit of a climb to get to Snow Mesa. I met up with High-5 along the way as he was breaking camp; we hiked together for a few miles.

Figure 138 - climbing up to Snow Mesa, looking behind at what we had just climbed

The Mesa had mildly rolling terrain before descending down a rocky trail to the pass. We passed a dried pond where Michael stayed the night. There was also a couple very slowly moving creeks along the way. High-5 stopped to get some water at one of these. I moved on; he would easily catch up with me later.

The view from the Mesa to the south and west was of the colorful San Juan Mountains. In a couple days I will be enjoying the heart of these mountains. The sight made me realize that after Lake City I would have only one more resupply stop before finishing the trail. This was almost over. I have only 130 more miles to go.

Along the Mesa I met up with Rabbit, Sudsie, Michael, Talus and Pablo, High-5, Heath Bar, and El Gato del Monte, and one other (I didn't get her name). We rested and talked a bit before making our descent.

Figure 139 - Snow Mesa below

I had a brief exchange on social media in the weeks prior to starting the hike with one of the crew that day, Sudsie. It was there that we discovered at least two Yoopers would be on the CT this year. There always seems to be a special bond for me with people I meet from back home; we are a rare breed; every encounter outside of the U.P. is worth celebrating. We are both voluntarily displaced in Colorado, and loving it. She's a student in Boulder. Yooper Land, you were well represented in the CT Class of 2018!

This picture of her has a trail story worth telling. Ultralight backpacking is the craze these days. Her hiking partners were coaching her on the trend, using her water bottle as an example. Her common, plastic, store-bought water bottle had a ring on the lid that serves no purpose after the seal is broken, so the advice was to remove it and save the weight... maybe a small fraction of an ounce. Yes, it's a thing. While taking off the ring she cut her finger. The picture is her holding her cut finger above her head, and maybe laughing a little about the ridiculous ultralight exercise.

Figure 140 - Sudsie nursing a wound (picture provided by Sudsie)

We all needed to get to the pass to catch a free shuttle into Lake City. A lady pulled up in a Volvo wagon and we squeezed seven stinky hikers with packs into it. The others got a hitch. I love these local folks - trail angels - willing to make sure us hikers are welcome.

I finished Segment 21 into Spring Creek Pass Trailhead for a total of 11.1 miles on the day and 1500 feet elevation gain before noon. My plan was to stay in Lake City a few days for a well needed rest. I was two and a half days ahead of schedule.

Lake City was wonderful. My feet needed a good rest and I needed to reset my schedule as to not mess up my plan to have Bobbi pick me up in Durango on a weekend. It would allow me to keep my hotel reservations in Durango and Bobbi wouldn't need to take time off of work to come and get me. I could have caught a bus or train back as an alternate plan.

It's exciting knowing I'm nearly finished with some of the

best scenery remaining. Going southbound is absolutely the best way for me; it has a slow start, gradual buildup, and a fabulous ending.

In trying to figure out my ride back to the trailhead, I didn't want to wait for the free ride because they wouldn't get me to the trail until about 1pm, just in time for the rain. The other options were to hitchhike or hire a shuttle. I decided that if I could find someone to share the cost of the shuttle I would do that. Richard, a guy I met at the hostel was a willing participant.

> **Pro Tip:** Unplug! Even when you are in town, minimize the use of everything except what is essential. I kept my phone and GPS powered off most of the time, even in town. I turned them on to send a check-in message to Bobbi and to check on my location maybe a couple times per day while on the trail. It was so great to be present and not distracted. Do it; it's super healthy to clear out all that noise.

I did my laundry while in town at a coin operated laundromat on the north end of town. It's close to a bakery. Go there; it's fantastic! I also received my resupply from Kristie who met me where I was staying.

I didn't need to see the medic for my blistered heels; they recovered fine without any special attention from a professional.

Although I very much enjoyed the peacefulness of this little town, I was absolutely ready to get back on the trail. Our shuttle left Lake City at 6:30am and we started the trail at 7. It was August 15th when I started Segment 22 at Spring Creek Pass Trailhead.

The morning presented a nice blue hue in the distant mountains and Snow Mesa where I had descended a few days before.

Figure 141 - Blue hue in the mountains behind us

Most of the early trail was following a jeep track, then a rocky single track up to Jaroda Mesa and then down to the area of the CT Friends Yurt.

Figure 142 - Jaroda Mesa

As I came into the area where the yurt is located, I heard the sounds of sheep - hundreds of sheep. A lone shepherd on horseback and his two faithful shepherd dogs kept them collected in the gulch. We also had a distant view of where we would be traveling tomorrow.

Figure 143 - Sheep herd near the yurt

I waited at the far side of the gulch for Richard for a bit and looked for a couple flat spots for our tents. I couldn't find anything that wasn't full of sheep manure. The other side of the gulch seemed worth a try, the side from where I had come, where the yurt was. Richard came along shortly after and we decided to check out the area near the yurt.

Figure 144 - CT Friends Yurt

We set up our tents as the first round of showers rolled in. The sun came out a little later, enough to dry the tents.

It didn't take long for us to check out the inside of the yurt, eventually deciding to stay in the yurt for the night. $20 a night seemed like a fair deal in exchange for a shelter with a stove, table, chairs, bunk beds, and an entertaining log book. We gathered some wood from the fallen trees around the shelter and started a crackling fire; it was toasty warm inside while it rained off and on outside. Great choice. Very cozy.

Figure 145 - The view from the deck of the Yurt

It wasn't a long day, on purpose. I wanted to start off slow, given I had been resting a few days. I put in 8.7 miles and 1700 feet elevation.

Sleeping in the yurt made for a quick start the next morning, not having the chore of taking down our tents and the convenience of a place out of the elements was nice too.

There was a mouse in the Yurt during the night, but it wasn't in my stuff so I didn't pay much attention to it. Others had written in the log book about the bothersome porcupines, so I can do a mouse.

The day would bring us to the highest point on the CT, another milestone day. But before we could reach that point we had several hills to climb, all above tree line, steady and mild throughout most of the day. It was another scenic day in the San Juan Mountains.

Figure 146 - Climbing up from the yurt through willows and switchbacks

Back on the trail I met this young lady named Shannon today. She had camped above tree line the night before. We would leap frog for much of the day.

Figure 147 - Shannon ahead of me on this portion of the trail

Figure 148 - Lake Fork Gunnison River Valley and San Juans

There wasn't much wildlife to be seen today. But I did get a visit from a curious long tailed weasel.

Figure 149 - Long Tailed Weasel

Figure 150 - King's Crown flowers next to the trail

We arrived at the highest point along the CT before lunch. Hats off to Richard! He started this hike solo and significantly overweight. He has stuck to it, lost some poundage, kick starting a healthier lifestyle - good on him!!

Figure 151 - Richard and I celebrating the highest point on the trail

Shannon is from Texas and is currently living in Colorado,

working with Job Corps on maintaining trails in Colorado. Shannon has a refreshing "making it work" approach to living and loving life.

> **Pro Tip:** Take pictures of the people you meet. This scenery is incredible... but that's only half the experience. The people you meet along the way are very likely going to be the most memorable part of your journey. Introduce yourself and have a conversation.

Figure 152 - Shannon at the highest point

Like yesterday, the rain and storms came, but not before we made our summit. It was nice not to be rushed off a summit.

A mile and a half beyond the highest point is Carson Saddle, the end of Segment 22. Seeing old mining remains near here brought with it the echoes of days gone by. They rushed to these beautiful hills for the dream of extracting hidden treasures and beginning a new exciting life. To gamble on the unknown and the wonder of the land is part of what draws all of us to come here, even today.

Figure 153 – Shannon and Richard approaching Carson Saddle

Figure 154 - Many of these marmots have been seen and heard

Half way up our last pass of the day the first storm hit. Thunder and lightning above and all around us, the rain steady and cold. I was with Richard. Shannon had moved ahead. We took cover as best we could in the willow brush. We were above tree line as we will be for most of the next couple days.

After 30 minutes or so I decided to head for the pass since

the weather was clearing in that direction. It was a little risky but I just wanted to get out of the cold wind and rain. It turned out OK, but I don't recommend trying to outsmart mother nature.

Figure 155 - The storm now behind us

Less than an hour later I was setting up camp at the un-named smaller lake above Cataract Lake with the threat of more storms looming. Again, just in time, I was able to get the tent up before it hit. Richard lagged a bit behind me and set up his camp below me as the weather turned bad. We didn't connect after this, as I was on the trail before him the next morning and moving faster. But I saw later that he had finished the trail a few days behind me. Yeah, Richard!

Figure 156 - Camp at the smaller lake above Cataract Lake

I read about using rocks to hold down URSacks in places without trees. This was a place for me to test that theory since there was nothing but short brush and plenty of marmots in the area who would be very happy to take my food. It worked as advertised, no pests bothered my food bag.

Figure 157 - URSack held down with rocks

It rained for nearly two hours. I was tired, so I ate a cold meal inside my tent, less than I would normally have for my evening meal and not the normal place I would be eating a meal. The rain and wind were cold, too cold and wet to eat outside. So, I put on several layers, cuddled up in my little home, and fell asleep to the sound of the rain, relaxed and comfortable.

Camp was at 5.5 miles into Segment 23. The total today was 14 miles and 3200 feet elevation gain.

The next day I was up at dawn and out on the trail before the sun broke over the mountains. I am solo again and looking forward to my destination for the day: Elk Creek headwaters. I've read much about the beauty of that area.

One thing I noticed about the San Juans compared to other places along this trail is that I feel so much smaller here. The views are expansive. It seems the mountains never end, but it's never the same view. Around each bend in the trail is another unique breathtaking view.

Figure 158 - Looking down into the Poll Creek Drainage

I had several highlights for the day. One of them was that I filtered water out of the headwaters of the Rio Grande River. I'm not sure why I didn't take any pictures here. Sometimes I get so caught up with where I am that I don't want to disturb the moment with the chore of taking pictures.

Figure 159 - Approaching the descent to the Rio Grande headwaters

A mile after crossing the Rio Grande I was at Stoney Pass Road, the end of Segment 23. There's a short uphill road walk before crossing the road and starting Segment 24 and also entering the Weminuche Wilderness Area.

A couple miles into this trail it intersects with Cunningham Gulch trail. It was here I met a guy with an amputated leg. He was retirement age and segment hiking alone, both ways (northbound and southbound). What a great motivational example he was! What an inspiration to accomplish big things in spite of obstacles and challenges. I really have no excuses now.

Another highlight of the day was a close encounter with a coyote. He crossed just a few feet in front of me. I yelled for him go away; he agreed; we're both happy. I recalled the night before I heard coyote on the other side of the lake from where I set up camp. They seemed very close to where Richard was camped.

Pro Tip: Coyote are pack animals, like dogs or wolves. If one approaches you don't run or turn your back, get big, get loud, wave your arms, and throw objects. If attacked, fight back. (Wildlife, Coyotes 2018)

Figure 160 - Notice the coyote up on the ridge

Figure 161 - Just another great view from the start of Segment 24

At 5.8 miles into Segment 24 the trail splits with the CDT. I missed the turnoff. Instead of following the CT, I continued on the CDT for a mile or so downhill. When I noticed I wasn't on my way to the Elk Creek Headwaters I had to back track. I really don't like these kinds of mistakes, especially when I'm low on energy and, once again, storms were gathering around me. So, in the rain I made the correction with the necessary elevation gain and began my descent of many switch backs toward Elk Creek. It was indeed as beautiful as I had seen in pictures, maybe more so.

Figure 162 - Looking down into the headwaters of Elk Creek

I camped near an old run down miners' cabin. When I say "run down" I mean one of the walls is being held up by a single board to brace the wall from falling over. Two walls are no longer standing and the roof is half caved in. A north-bound hiker was staying inside this thing for the night, and he lit a small fire in there. Like I've said before, there are all kinds of people on the trail.

My feet were cold, as my shoes were wet from the rain. I don't sleep well when my feet are cold. I'm above 12,000 feet again too, so it will be chilly. It was indeed a double socks kind of night.

I made it to mile 7.2 of Segment 24, another 20-mile day with my little detour and over 4000 feet elevation gain.

Truly this place is an inexhaustible study. The variety of forests, abundant fields, millions of individually distinct rocks, trees of all shapes and sizes, a near infinite inventory of flora, wildlife from moose to the tiniest of insects, mountainscapes of magnificent proportion, billions of stars in the night skies, sounds ranging from deafening silence to crashing thunder and blustery winds, clouds of ever-changing shapes and patterns, rains and storms, lakes, creeks, and waterfalls that sing and speak in their own native language ... it all fully engages and even overloads the senses, at times to the point of bringing a person to tears. When I begin to catalog all I've experienced on this trail, it's overwhelming. It's why I still have a hard time answering simple questions like, "how was your hike?"

CHAPTER NINE

Elk Creek Headwaters to
Southern Terminus

T here are two ways for me to consider a rainbow in the morning. I could see a promise that God won't flood me out, or I could see it as a sign of rain ahead. I went with the promise theme because today was my last day before resupply and I was about to enter into the last leg of this great adventure. Remain positive!

Figure 163 - Promises, promises

It started raining just as I was ready to get out of camp. So far the promise thing wasn't working out.

I didn't feel much like packing up in the rain, so I held off until it stopped, about a half hour. Being wet and cold was getting old. Let this be a dryer day.

> **Pro Tip:** Placing everything in waterproof bags will help make the cold, wet days a little more tolerable. You don't want your electronics to get wet nor your first aid kit. Wet toilet paper will force an unwelcome bought of creativity. You definitely don't want your down sleeping bag to get wet or your dry set of clothes to get soaked. And getting your food wet could be a caloric disaster. General rule: when in doubt, put it in a plastic bag.

I had heard about how dicey the upper part of Elk Creek was going to be. Sure enough, the stories didn't disappoint. It was loose wet talus on a narrow trail, a steep drop to the creek on one side and a wall of granite on the other. It wasn't long but it was memorable.

Figure 164 - Loose and steep down Elk Creek

Just down this grade, still not in in trees, a lady was camping near the edge of the creek. She had just risen out of her tent, all bundled up in her puffy. It must have been chilly in this canyon.

Soon I was below tree line with White Dome fading behind me.

Figure 165 - White Dome

At mile 11.6 the trail runs by the shore of a pond with both Vestal and Arrow Peaks reflecting in the water... postcard beautiful!

Figure 166 - Vestal and Arrow Peaks reflecting in the pond

The descent follows a very nicely flowing creek, angry at times. But soon the trail separates from the creek into a quiet forest and then down to the Animas River where a train track runs parallel. The trail crosses the tracks. It's the still active narrow gauge line that runs between Durango and Silverton.

Figure 167 - Narrow gage line between Durango and Silverton

The train went by as I approached. The conductor sounded the train whistle. It echoed through the canyon much like I had seen and heard in old west films. For a moment I wondered if it was a message from my late father cheering me on to finish. He was a railroad agent for 42 years. I know it sounds crazy, but I don't believe anything happens by coincidence. I'm sure the train blows it's whistle here every day. But that I was in this place at this time on this journey, hearing the whistle blow while thinking about my dad when it blew is admittedly not an everyday occurrence. There are unexplainable, overwhelming, and emotional moments on the trail. This was one for me.

I took a quick break under a generous pine tree near the Elk Park rail stop as it started to rain again. A day-hiking couple joined me. We made small talk and within a few minutes the rain subsided. I headed up the trail a short distance to the edge of Molas Creek for a quick water stop and snack. Then I started the 1800-foot climb to Molas Pass where I would be staying at Molas Pass campground for a zero day and resupply.

Figure 168 - Climbing up toward Molas Pass, the Animas River Valley starting to fade behind me

Rain had been falling off and on throughout the day, but the sky was beginning to clear and by the time I reached Molas Lake the skies were brilliant blue. I was eager to set up camp and enjoy the rest of the day by the lake.

Figure 169 - Approach to Molas Pass. The skies breaking.

There was no cell service again so I used my Garmin to let Bobbi know I had arrived safely at the campground. I then sent a note to Pagosa and Kristie, making final arrangements for my re-supply. Kristie would be here in the morning as Larry had come down with the flu. Poor guy doesn't catch a break.

Figure 170- Camp at Molas Lake

After setting up my tent I lay inside, hot and dry. I loved it. My feet were finally able to dry. It will be a zero-day tomorrow.

And there you have it. Remember the rainbow in the morning? Believe in the promise!

It wasn't long before I headed to the small store at the camp ground office to get some tokens for a shower. They didn't have laundry facilities so I took a couple clothes items into the shower with me to wash them. I then laid the items out on my picnic table for drying.

I had dinner with a gorgeous view, again. There's no better place I'd rather have a rehydrated meal. What a treat!

The day was light, 11.5 miles and just under 2000 feet elevation gain.

> **Pro Tip:** Keep a journal. There are so many precious details that will be forgotten if you don't write them down while you are on the trail. I did my journaling every night before I went to sleep. I'm so glad I did; it's a big part of the content of this book. I can always relive these days by simply reading any page of the journal.

The next day, Aug 19th, I showered again, watched the osprey dive for trout, charged my batteries, received my resupply, had a root beer, ate a bean and cheese burrito (from Kristie), had an ice cream bar from the camp office, dropped some extra food items off at the hiker box, and relaxed in the tent while watching fishermen float around on the lake. It was a beautiful sunny day. It felt like a true zero day.

My camp neighbors invited me over for some s'mores and a beer around their campfire. It's hard to refuse that kind of generosity. The couple and their three children were from north of Denver doing it right with their children in the outdoors. Thinking back when I was a boy, camping with the family are special memories. I know their kids won't forget this either.

And who knows, they may find themselves on a long trail some-day thinking back to when their parents took them on camping trips.

Enough of all this relaxing! The next day I was on the trail before the campground started stirring, solo still.

It was a cold morning with ice on the inside of my tent and frost on the outside. Sleeping 20 feet away from a lake at over 10,000 feet makes for a great picture, but it isn't the best conditions for tent camping. The lake keeps it cool and humid. I had nearly full ventilation on both sides of the tent; it didn't seem to reduce the condensation much. So, I put on my rain gloves to keep my hands from getting wet and freezing, packed up the gear, and off I went. I was on the trail at 6:40.

Shortly after crossing Molas Pass, near Little Molas Lake, I passed a pine cone throwing squirrel. Not very hospitable, but I kindly thanked him for the pleasure of passing through his home.

Segment 24 was behind me now. Segment 25 begins.

Figure 171 - Molas Pass road crossing

Figure 172 - Little Molas Lake

After an 800 foot climb I checked my phone to see that I had service. So, I gave Bobbi a quick call. It had been a few days since I had service and I had heard her voice. I remember talking to her about how excited I was to have picked up my last resupply and that I was going to finish. I was on my way home.

Figure 173 - Not a bad place to have cell service. Little Molas Lake below.

The landscape is changing again. The full colors of the San Juans are now in clear view and close up, what I had seen a couple days prior. The reds, rusts, greys, and even some blues and green hues can be seen in the rocks that make up these mountains and paint the land.

Figure 174 - It's like an old west movie. The San Juans once again do not disappoint

The trail twists around these hills, keeping Lime Creek drainage to my left for most of the morning. Several bikers passed me; we made quick conversation. A small group of backpackers were breaking camp near the trail a couple miles up from the pass.

Figure 175 - Twin Sisters off to the right - 13,000 foot peaks

One biker from Utah stopped just below the pass south of Rolling Mountain to admire the landscape. We talked about the lack of flowers but were astonished at the beauty in the colored and varying shapes of the hills and mountains in this area. He had biked here before and felt it worthy to return.

Figure 176 - Colorful even without flowers

A few miles after crossing another unnamed pass and the intersection with Rico-Silverton Trail, I had arrived at my camp for the night - Cascade Creek. As the name suggests, there are many small water falls along this creek.

Three others arrived about the same time but they were moving on to camp later on in the Segment. Honey went for a quick dip in the very cold creek. Tito's bum knee was making him noticeably uncomfortable, he went on ahead thinking the others would catch up. Golden Grahams and I talked gear. I showed him the poles I had been testing. We both had Gossamer packs.

Figure 177 - Cascade Creek

Throughout the day I kept thinking, "only five days left". And now as I lay in my tent, I'm thinking I only have 4 more days before this is finished. What an incredible journey! But it's almost over. Happy and sad at the same time.

> **Pro Tip:** Some people bring a koozie to keep their food warm while rehydrating. So did I until it ripped. Then I started using my insulated skull cap. It works great! The cap was also used as a hot pad to take my pot off my stove when the han-

dle was hot. I guess as long as a person doesn't have to wear it at the same time, this could be a nice multipurpose piece of clothing to save a little weight.

Today I finished Segment 24 and hiked 14.8 miles of Segment 25 for a total of 16.3 miles and 2500 feet elevation gain.

The next day was a largely uneventful day. Lots of ups and downs and less dramatic views, but still great mountain scenery.

There are several different ways the trail is marked. Most of the time there are triangle shaped CT metal markers nailed to trees. Sometimes the trees are marked with an "i". Other times the CT log is carved into maker poles.

Figure 178 - Follow the i

Figure 179 - Another saddle crossing

Figure 180 - Long morning shadows on soft rolling hills

The trail twists across a fire service road several times before reaching Celebration Lake at the end of Segment 25. This is near Bolam Pass and it's where I caught up with Golden Grahams, Honey, and Tito. Tito mentioned his knee felt much better. They were just chillin' next to the lake, not wanting this hike to be over.

Figure 181 - Celebration Lake

A couple miles past Celebration Lake and into Segment 26 the trail passes Hermosa Peak. I took a quick break just below this peak to enjoy the view.

Figure 182 - Hermosa Peak 12,579 feet

There was a small saddle and Blackhawk Pass to go over today, neither were incredibly demanding. Both had great views.

Figure 183 - Labeled "small saddle" in the Databook

Figure 184 - Blackhawk Pass

The weather was mostly cloudy and the temp was cool. The trail was mostly below tree line.

I made a stop at Straight Creek before setting up camp. It will be the last reliable water source for 22 miles.

And, of course, a storm rolled through just as I was looking for a place to camp. I pitched my tent between two towering pines. The squirrels had fun tossing pine cones at the tent for a while.

There were a few north-bound hikers that passed today. Not much conversation except a quick wish of luck to them. They all seemed tired. Going northbound on the CT is a much tougher start with twice as much elevation gain in the first 20 miles compared to the beginning of a southbound route.

I saw the Utah biker again. He stopped with me to rest just below the last pitch of the day. I was running low on Ibuprofen, which after a little hint, he offered up some of his to me. Of course, I graciously accepted the offer. My back was still bothering me.

Only three more trail days left!

It rained most of the night and it was cold and wet most of the next day. My shoes were soaked, my tent was wet and dirty and most of my clothes and body was dirty and stinky. This was not my favorite day on the trail. I did my best to clean up in my tent in an attempt to take the edge off this downer mood I was in. These are the times when mental toughness matters. The ability to look beyond the temporal and settle the mind on the bigger picture is what can turn these discontent moments into enough hope to push through to better days, which will surely come.

I have come to gain a full realization that great experiences don't necessarily imply that every moment is great. There are parts of this thru-hiking experience I do not like. I do not like being dirty and stinky all the time. I do not like being wet for days on end. I do not like putting on dirty clothes. Whereas, thru-hikers often embrace being called a "dirtbag", I hold some disdain for the "dirtbagness" aspect of this kind of existence. Great experiences are great because the high times far outweigh the low times. And this has been the case for me on the CT.

I did get a chance to talk with Bobbi today and I checked the weather forecast. Tomorrow should be clearing in the late morning. It should be at least partly sunny for most of the day and through Friday. Sunny and dry is a great way to end this journey, for sure!

Some of the views today were interesting with fog and mist in and through the valleys and ridges. I was forest walking today with occasional views from on top of ridges. There were areas where the trees were decorated with Spanish moss. It was damp and dank, mystical and enchanting.

This is in stark contrast to the very dry spring and early summer in the San Juans this year. The rain of these most recent weeks helped slow the progress of the 416 and Bruno fires not far from here. The 416 Fire which was the sixth-largest wildfire in Colorado history (Mitchell 2018). The San Juan National Forest and CT were closed from June 12th to July 12th. (Simonovich 2018) (Ruble 2018)

Despite the current rainy situation, I'm so happy the rains came so I could enjoy this time and this place.

Figure 185 - Misty morning in the valleys

Figure 186 - Hiking through drifting clouds

Figure 187 - Looks like the skies are breaking

Around 6pm a fellow CT hiker, Ron, joined me in camp. He's about my age. He had planned on the same schedule as I did, giving me a hiking partner for the rest of the trip. I had been a little apprehensive about stories of an active mountain lion in the last Segment - active meaning the cat has shown little fear of humans, several reported close encounters. That Ron came along at this time, is that coincidence? I don't think so. Some would say, "The trail provides". All I know for sure is that I appreciate the serendipitous nature of this trail, and I'll feel better hiking with another person to the end.

Honey, Tito, Golden Grahams, a young British lady, and a guy from South Carolina (I'll refer to this group as "The Running Crew" for reasons that will become evident later) set up their camp nearby. We heard them below us as we walked out on a bench (an elevated narrow flat feature) to check out the view we had read about in The Colorado Trail Databook. There are a few great camp sites along this short path too. We enjoyed the views of the surrounding hills with the clouds breaking, offering a glimmer of hope for better weather on our finishing days. Some low hanging clouds were rising as the sun set for the day.

> **Pro Tip:** When selecting a tent site don't just look down for flat spots, look up for dead trees or limbs that could pose a danger of falling on your tent in windy conditions.

Figure 188 - View from the bench

I had only two more days, and only one more rehydrated

dinner before rejoining the rest of civilization!

I finished Segment 26 and hiked 12.3 miles of Segment 27 for a total of 14.2 miles and 2100 feet elevation gain on the day.

> **Pro Tip:** Cooking in freezer bags is convenient and easy. Putting meals in freezer bags cuts the amount of packaging you'll need to carry, and if you're resourceful enough you can reuse the freezer bags. You won't need cooking pots and you won't need to clean them up; just heat up some water, pour it into the bag, let it cook in your koozie, and then eat out of the bag with a long spork.

The next day started off much like the day before with clouds and fog as I made my way up the Highline Trail (or Indian Trail Ridge). At first I was alone, because I had left before Ron. But about half way along the ridge I was joined by The Running Crew.

Figure 189 - Low hanging clouds to start the day

Figure 190 - I took a short rest here before gaining Indian Ridge Trail

Figure 191 - The clouds started to break along Indian Ridge Trail

About the time The Running Crew caught up with me, the fog lifted and the skies began to break. We took a short break and talked about how we wanted the trail to be longer; no one wanted this to end.

Near one of the rolling summits I met a guy and a lady out

day hiking. The guy had an amputated leg - the second time on this trail I've seen an amputee hiker. It was another motivating event.

I filled up on water and had lunch at Taylor Lake. It was probably the most enjoyable lunch I've had on the trail. A beautiful setting, the sun drifting in and out between the clouds, and a cool breeze blowing put a smile on my face, a near perfect formula.

Figure 192 - Taylor Lake

I then continued to Kenebeck Trailhead, a mile up the trail, where I met up with The Running Crew again. And now you'll understand why I've called them The Running Crew: they wanted to run to Durango from here (20 miles) to get steak and beer for dinner.

A short time later the amputee guy shows up at his truck and in a few minutes he agreed to take The Running Crew backpacks to the trailhead. So The Running Crew with a couple snacks and some water was off, running to Durango. I took a picture before they left. They asked me to join them. I kindly refused, offering some comment about my less capable older bones.

Figure 193 - The Running Crew (from left: Golden Grahams, Tito, Carolina guy, Honey, British lady)

I continued down the trail, first pausing at the trailhead sign. It was the start of the final Segment of the trail, Segment 28. I thought about Pagosa, how he should be here with me to enjoy this feeling. So, I called him up and told him as much. It was a reflective time for me: sad that Pagosa wasn't here, happy because I was about to achieve something amazing, retrospective as I recalled all it took to get here and the new friends I've made along the way.

Figure 194 - The final segment trailhead sign, Segment 28

A few minutes later Ron appears, coming down the trail to meet me as Pagosa and I were finishing our conversation. We both reflected on those who were our greatest supporters, those whom we utterly could not have done this trail without. Our immediate families topped the list. Our eyes were glassy as we were feeling incredibly grateful and blessed to be here, our hearts were full. We hiked the rest of the day together. The plan was to hike like this tomorrow and finish together as well.

Figure 195 – Ron in the talus on the other side of Kennebec Pass

We're camped next to Junction Creek. Several more thru-hikers passed by. We were all beginning to celebrate, even a day early. Anticipation was in the air; we were just hours away from the finish line. Fourteen more miles tomorrow and that's it. The end of my CT thru-hike is one meal away. It's been amazing in so many ways.

Today I finished Segment 27 and hiked 7.1 miles into Segment 28, for a total of 15.4 miles and 1700 feet elevation gain.

The next day, on August 24th, 2018, I finished hiking the Colorado Trail! In some respects, it felt like any other zero day because I looked forward to a hot shower and "real" food. But beyond this zero day there was to be another zero day, and then another.

The finality of it as I approached the last mile was starting to sink in. I didn't push myself these past few days. I set my scheduled and stuck to it. I'm glad I did because I had more time to mentally and emotionally prepare for my approach to this final trailhead.

Figure 196 - Ron taking some of our final steps

Ron and I finished strong. His wife and children were there to meet him with a big banner and big hugs. He had been section hiking this trail for seven years; this was his finisher. I let him go first to take in the moment with his wife and kids.

A couple minutes later I touched the trailhead sign. It was final. I had finished hiking the Colorado Trail!

I laid my pack down knowing full well that I wouldn't be putting it on and walking the next day. It felt heavy this time in spite of it actually be the lightest it's ever been without days of food and liters of water.

A few celebratory pictures and some small talk while taking down a beer was a perfect ending. Like most big moments in my life, it was just a small space in time. But it was one of pure satisfaction and one I would remember forever.

Then it was time to leave the trail. They took me to my hotel, I cleaned up, called Bobbi, then I went out for a nice dinner where I enjoyed another beer, pretzel sticks with white cheddar sauce for an appetizer, ahi tuna steak for the entre, and peach cobbler for dessert. Yes, I ate it all.

It's starting to feel like I'm back. Tomorrow I will need to start being and doing as I was and did 41 days ago, except maybe with a few changes the trail has offered me.

Figure 197 - Celebrating the moment at the southern terminus.

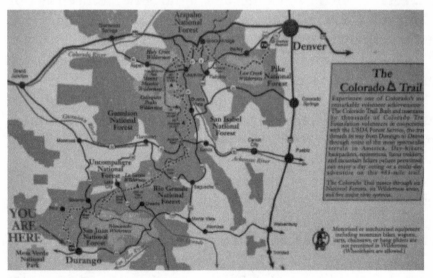

Figure 198 - A map of the trail

CHAPTER TEN

Gear List

Below is a list of gear items I took with me on the CT with approximate weights. This list came about through an exhaustive exercise of research and trials. Many of the choices are so closely comparable. Gear companies are very competitive on many levels. But in the end for many of my choices it was more about what felt right, a gut feeling.

I spent a great deal of time on the big-three: pack, shelter, and sleeping system. A person needs to be comfortable walking all day, so the right pack is essential. The shelter becomes home; scrutinize it for comfort, functionality, and weight. And the sleeping system is an important element in recharging the spirit every day. Getting any one of these wrong could make or break a long hike.

Pack - Gossamer Mariposa 60 - 37oz

Shelter
- Tent - Zpacks Duplex - 21oz
- Stakes - Boundless Voyage Titanium V-Shaped Nail Tent Stakes Ultralight - 3.2oz

Sleeping System
- Quilt - Loco Libre Gear 20° Operator Series Ghost Pepper Topquilt - 18oz

- Pad - Sea to Summit UltraLight Insulated Mat - 17.4oz
- Pillow - Klymit X large pillow - 2.9oz
- Light Thermals (night) - Duofold Mid Weight Wicking Thermal Pant - 6oz
- Long Sleeve Shirt (night) - Thermowave Merino Xtreme Merino Wool Performance Base Layer 200 GSM - 6.8oz
- Night Socks - Possumdown Possum and Merino Wool Bushman's Friend Sock - 3.1oz

Clothing

- Rain Coat - The Packa - rain/wind coat and pack cover - 10.5oz
- Rain Pants - Outdoor Research Men's Helium Pants - 5.7oz
- Rain Mitts - Mountain Laurel Designs eVent Rain Mitts - 1.5oz
- Extra Socks - Darn Tough Hike-Trek Merino Wool Micro Crew Cushion Sock - 2.2oz
- Extra sock liners - Injinji liners - 1.2oz
- Puffy Jacket - Patagonia Nano Puff Jacket - 11.9oz
- Camp shirt - 8.4oz
- Gloves - Running Sports Gloves - 1.9pz
- Cold Hat - Mountain Hardware Caelum Dome Beanie - 2oz
- Clothes Sack - zPacks Food Dry Bag - 1.6oz

Personal Care

- Trowel - The Tentlab Deuce of Spades Backcountry Potty Trowel - .6oz
- First Aid Kit - Small assortment of ointments, bandages, optional meds (like an antidiarrheal) - 2.9oz
- Bandana - Pendleton Men's Jumbo Bandana, Warrior Rock Navy - 1.6oz
- Toothbrush - Compact, something like the BCB Adventure Folding Toothbrush - .7
- Consumables: floss, toothpaste, camp soap, Gold Bond powder, toilet paper, Repel bug spray, meds,

laundry soap, sunscreen

Electronics
- Charger - Anker PowerCore II 10000 - 6.8oz
- Camera Charger - 2.4oz
- GPS/Communicator - Garmin Inreach Explorer+ - 8.8oz
- Carried in a fanny pack: Camera spare battery, Sony a6000 w/16-50mm lens, camera remote control, dual wall plug w/2 cords, tripod

Kitchen/Hydration
- Spork - Tritan Spork with Full-Sized Spoon, Fork and Serrated Knife Edge - .4oz
- Water Purification - MSR Guardian Purifier - 22oz
- Stove - MSR PocketRocket - 3oz
- Cup - 750ml Titanium Outdoor Camping Pot Cooking - 4.4oz
- Oil containers - empty for olive oil - .7oz
- Food Koozie - homemade from reflective blanket - 1.6oz
- Wind Shield - Docooler Ultralight Ultra-thin Titanium Outdoor Camping Stove Wind Shield Screen Windproof Plate - .7oz
- Food Bags - LOKSAK Opsak Barrier 12 X 20 - 3.1oz
- Hanging Bag - Ursack MAJOR S29.3 All White Bear Resistant Sack Bag - 9oz
- Water Bottle - empty Smartwater bottle - 1oz
- Water Blatter - Platypus Platy Bottle, 2.0-Liter and 1-Liter - 2.3oz

Misc
- Fire Starter - 2 mini lighters - 1.3oz
- Headlamp - Energizer Vision HD+ LED Headlamp - 3.1oz
- Knife - Gerber Ripstop I Knife, Serrated Edge - 2.2oz
- Cord - 50' zPacks Z line slick chord - .9oz
- Colorado Trail Databook - portion - 1.5oz

CHAPTER ELEVEN

COMMON QUESTIONS

I n the weeks and months following my hike I've had many questions and conversations about what it was like. It's difficult to describe to people who have never experienced life on the trail. Usually my answers were a feeble attempt to find the right words that could do it justice. And now as I've attempted to write it all down, I'm still struggling and I've very likely missed the mark in some cases. And I'm quite certain that no matter how much time or effort I put into this I'll still fall short.

Nonetheless, I found it necessary to include a chapter that covers some of the most common questions I've been asked. Here are a few of them.

<u>Would you do it again? Are you planning another long hike?</u>

When I first got off the trail I wasn't all that excited about doing it again; I wasn't opposed to it, but I knew I needed to think about it. This kind of thing is tough in every way. I missed my home and family. I missed a lot of things. But, yet I still felt that I did the right thing and that this was undeniable part of who I am, that I was meant to do this.

So after some weeks had passed and I had time to process the entirety of it all, I believe I have the answer to this question. And the answer is yes; I believe another adventure like this is in my future. I'm not sure when, but I'd like to head out again. I'm not sure where. It may be that I'll do the Long Trail in Vermont, the John Muir Trail in the High Sierras in northern California, the Arizona Trail, or maybe I'll take a few years to section hiking the Pacific Crest Trail. I don't have much of an appetite for the Appalachian Trail, and the Continental Divide Trail seems a little overwhelming. Bobbi and I have some other things planned in 2019. So, maybe 2020 or maybe later.

Do you still keep in contact with people you met on the trail?

I'm a believer that it's the people on the trail that make it so memorable and enjoyable. I've stayed in touch over social media with several of the people I met on the trail and who are mentioned in this book. The shared experience of the trail will always be our common bond. And who knows, we may meet up on the trail again. Some of them live here in CO so it would be especially convenient for us to plan a weekend hike or something longer. It would be great to catch up. The Colorado Trail Foundation also has events; I may see them at one of those events. Or it will be just as sweet to have them linger in my memory of this special time in my life.

How much weight did you loose on the trail?

I've always been slender. But as I get older it gets harder to stay that way. I didn't have a whole lot to lose when I started the trail but I still ended up dropping around 15 pounds. And it felt GREAT! It's just very difficult to carry the amount of food it would take to replace the calories burned every day. And it's even harder to eat that much food. I've heard it said that men tend to lose more weight on thru-hikes. I think the greatest factor is probably a question around who has more weight to lose. Anyone who exerts this much energy is bound to trim down at least a little.

How did your gear work out for you?

I spent a lot of time researching and trying out gear before the hike. It paid off. I used all the gear I brought with me and was extremely happy with the performance, with a few exceptions.

I made my own food koozie. A koozie is an insulated bag that helps keep food warm. About two thirds of the way through the hike it was wearing out and became ineffective. It was made from an insulated blanket I took home from a past hospital stay. If I should need another one, I may create one out of different materials or I may buy one. But I definitely would take it again.

My sleeping quilt was nice but it would have been nicer to have one that was a little longer and wider, and on a few nights I could have used a higher rated one. I had the 20 degree; maybe a 15 or 10-degree quilt would have been a little more comfortable for me. I sleep cold. People who don't sleep cold would probably be OK with a 20-degree sleeping bag or quilt.

The wind shield for my stove is super light, which is what I wanted. But what I didn't realize was that the wind has a tendency to toss it around more than I liked. It just wasn't very sturdy in the wind. Next time I may take a more stable one or invest in something like an MSR Reactor stove system.

I won't bring Loksak Opsak Barrier bags again. I brought them along because of their purported claim to seal in odors, thereby keeping curious animals away. Every one of them ripped near the seal, making them un-sealable and rendering them no more useful than a normal and much cheaper plastic freezer bag.

Again, I was very satisfied with a great majority of my gear choices. I recommend everyone do their own research to be sure what is brought on the trail won't fail them and will help maintain a comfortable weight category.

What would you do differently?

I'm actually quite pleased with my planning effort and how it all worked out. That's not to say that I did everything perfectly or that I wouldn't change a few things. But, overall, I had no epic failures, I did the things I wanted to do, and I feel that I fairly represented my purpose for being on the trail.

One thing I might change is to be less driven by my itinerary. Of course, there has to be some planning because resupplies don't happen on their own and the family needs to have some expectation of my return. But I found that every day I would remind myself of how I was progressing against the plan I had made. My day would then be measured at least to some degree against that expectation. I didn't make it a big deal, but it was still in the back of my mind. Maybe next time I'll set fewer daily expectations and just let the day govern itself more.

I may want to try different hiking patterns. I always hiked all day with a few short rests and got to camp by midafternoon. I would like to try something different, like taking a longer midday break and hiking until early evening. Of course, this would depend on the terrain. And taking a long midday break above tree line with summer monsoonal weather patterns wouldn't work every day. But, there is opportunity to change it up a little.

How were the bugs?

It was a dry year in Colorado and so the conditions were less favorable for bug proliferation. Being a Yooper I can very comfortably say that after experiencing Colorado over the past 20 years, there are no bug problems here. I have had a few exceptions, but generally speaking, it's all good.

I did have some encounters with ants. I don't like ants. We passed by some very large ant hills in the Lost Creek area. The ants were mostly in the northern part of the trail. But they didn't bite. So, it's worth noting but it wasn't bad. However, I do recommend careful tent placement with respect to ant colonies.

The other pests were flies around the Cataract Creek area on the south drainage of Peak 6 out of Breckenridge but before Camp Hale. If you recall from earlier, we intended on camping near the creek but were chased away by the flies.

Mosquitoes were minimal. I didn't use any bug spray or my bug head net the whole time on the trail.

I did, however, spray my clothes and gear with permethrin a few days before starting the trail. This helps keep insects away, primarily ticks, chiggers, and mosquitoes. As the instructions indicate, do not apply this directly on your skin. It's powerful stuff that maintains efficiency even after several washes.

Did is rain much?

I've documented the rain and the threat of rain throughout this book. Summer in Colorado means monsoonal weather patterns. It's common for clouds to roll in and for storms to hit the high country every afternoon. This was my experience. Some days it would rain on me and on other days it would rain around me. I don't think I was the target, but some days I wondered.

Colorado rain isn't typically an all-day affaire. It's not like other places where it rains without ceasing for days on end. So we have that going for us in Colorado.

Come prepared with the right gear and you shouldn't have any serious issues with the rain in Colorado. I've been told that there are no bad weather days, just bad choices in clothing. So, a person could adopt that thinking too.

How did you deal with wild animals?

I had people recommend that I should carry a firearm with me on the trail. I must say that I didn't see a single person with a firearm, nor did I hear of any animal attacks that would have required a firearm. It is well documented that firearms are predominantly unnecessary, that there are other usually more effective and less dangerous means of fending off critters in the wild. And this is true for most places in America.

On this hike I had close encounters with moose, dear, elk, coyote, cattle, horse, fox, dogs, mountain sheep, Dorset sheep, and a variety of rodents and birds. I also had a distant encounter with a large bear. In every case I used recommended encounter techniques to keep myself and the animals safe.

The wilderness can present dangerous situations with animals, no doubt. Getting between a mother and their offspring can be dangerous. Walking into a fresh kill can be dangerous. Cornering an animal can be dangerous. But all of these are extremely rare, mostly preventable, and each have proven methods and techniques for deescalating.

It's definitely worth some time studying how to act during an encounter. Each type of animal should be treated differently but in every case one should exercise the utmost respect. I've documented some of the more common ones in my Pro Tips throughout this book.

CHAPTER TWELVE

Afterthoughts

While on the trail it's difficult to understand the experience as a whole because most of each day is spent doing what the trail requires for that day and being more in the moment. Time for reflection comes after the trail is complete. It's good to let it rest and settle in for a while before coming to any conclusions about the experience. For me it's been a time for processing and discovering the most valuable and impactful lessons to carry forward with me in my life off the trail. These are some thoughts I had in the weeks following that final day arriving in Durango.

Journal It

It doesn't take long for the details of the trail experience to fade. Wouldn't it be nice to have it all recorded? This is why I recommend hikers keep a journal. It helps record daily trail activities, details that would otherwise be lost over time, emotions, people, trail conditions, milestones, thoughts, and anything worth remembering. It's good to look back to remember and relive.

I didn't start penning this book until 90 days after I had returned from the CT. The details in this book would have been lost if I had not kept a journal.

The Value of Time

Rick Warren, the author of *The Purpose Driven Life*, talks about the commodity of time. "Time is your most precious gift... you can't make more time... your time is your life... the greatest gift you can give someone is your time." I've had many thoughts about time since my return from the trail. Where in my life can I spend my time more purposefully and wisely on more important things to get and give the greatest value out of my remaining days? How I spend my time seems to matter more to me now more than ever.

Less on Things

The trail is great for demonstrating what few things we actually need to survive and be happy. It gave me a perspective on the essentials: food, water, shelter, clothing, and relationships. Everything else is either stuff to support me obtaining those essentials or it's just unnecessary fluff. When we buy stuff we give a portion of our life to it. If we buy a smart phone, TV, car, toys, etc. we sacrifice our time and energy to it so that it returns some value to us. This is time and energy lost to other potentially more important things that have greater intrinsic value – like, family and friends, gaining knowledge, volunteering, or fulfilling whatever purpose we have for our life. So, I've begun to question every purchase and I find it easier to resist the temptation to get stuff I don't need, stuff that robs me from the important things.

Happiness is Key

I don't recall where, but I read an interview of a high level executive who when asked about what keeps him at his job. He said there are two things that keep him at his job: that he's learning something and that he's happy. Since then I've adopted that philosophy for many areas of my life. I had an appreciation for this kind of thinking before my CT hike, but the trail has put an exclamation point on it. Never before has happiness been a greater priority for me. Since arriving in Durango I've become quite diligent at abandoning things in my life that don't bring me happiness. I simply don't want unhappiness or negativity in my life. I've avoided watching the news on TV. I walk away from people who dwell on negativity. I would rather be part of light to the world than be a party to those who seek to contribute to the darkness.

Hot Showers Are Great

I've always enjoyed a hot shower, but never more than I have since I left the trail. I'll just stand in the hot water appreciating every second, not wanting to get out. It's a minor struggle to shut it off and get out. I am probably still appreciating the act of being clean. Sometimes it's the simplest things that make me feel good.

Dirty Clothes

My dirty clothes basket fills up slower since I've been back. Whereas before the hike I would put on a clean set of clothes every day, I now find that I am wearing some articles of clothes several days without washing. If I didn't sweat too much or stain a shirt, I'll just put it back among my other clean cloths instead of washing it after one use. This is how my parents lived their whole lives. They grew up during the Great Depression, which gave them a different perspective on the value of what this more modern age takes for granted. Living less wasteful demonstrates our appreciation for how blessed we really are. I am now more mindful of where I can be less wasteful.

Final Thoughts

I'd like to thank everyone who encouraged me to take this trek, who supported me along the way, and who continue to challenge me to fulfill my purpose in a greater and more meaningful way every day. I hope everyone who reads this book finds the courage and drive to discover and pursue their purpose. I hope you all will begin or continue to take steps toward fulfilling that thing you were meant to be. In this I believe we are all connected. In this I believe we all will make the greatest impact on our world and experience the greatest blessing of life.

CHAPTER THIRTEEN

The Collegiate East - 2020

I like a nice yard. But just mowing isn't enough for me. The trim work needs to be done as well. And any noticeable grass clippings need to be raked up or swept off the sidewalk. To be done right, a task needs to be completely done.

Cleaning the car isn't just taking it through the automatic car wash. It needs to be cleaned on the inside too. Cleaning the car means washing the outside, vacuuming the inside, washing the windows, and wiping down the vinyl surfaces with the proper kinds of cleaners. Let's do it right. Let's do the whole job.

My hike of the Colorado Trail in 2018 was nothing short of life changing. Sure, I announced to the world that I finished hiking the trail. I started at the northern terminus at Waterton Canyon near Denver, maintained a continuous foot path on an official route, and 485 miles later I finished at the southern terminus in Durango. Having done that, every person I know accepts that I hiked the entire Colorado Trail.

On some level I probably accepted that fact too. But I also felt that there was something missing; I didn't feel completely accomplished. In 2018 I took the Western Collegiate Alternate Route, which means I didn't take the original Eastern Collegiate Route. Either route is fine. They are both equally official routes. Pick one and do it. There's no need to do both, unless you're me.

The route I didn't hike made it seem like I missed something. It felt unfinished. Something inside me for the past two years was nagging me to finish hiking that trail. Like mowing my yard or cleaning my car, I needed to do this right. I needed to go back to hike the Eastern Collegiate Route. And so I did that. I finished hiking the Colorado Trail, completely.

On Saturday, July 11th, my wife dropped me off at the eastern end of Twin Lakes near the dam. I wouldn't see her again until seven days later at Monarch Pass.

The eastern and western routes start at a trail junction about half-way along the southern shore of the reservoir. It was from here that I officially began my hike.

Along this first small segment before I arrived at the trail intersection, I saw a familiar Colorado Trail / Continental Divide Trail marker. I paused to take a picture and gaze at it. A rush of warm nostalgic memories from two years prior washed through me. These two trails share the same path for 200 miles along some of the most scenic in Colorado. My energy was instantly boosted. My life of just a mile ago was shedding fast. I was back on the trail again!

Figure 199 Once again on the CT / CDT

Some CT hikers muse on the difference between the eastern and western routes, suggesting that the east is merely a green tunnel to be endured, and the west is a grand alpine experience with epic views. Having hiked portions of the eastern route on many of my treks to summit these Collegiate Peaks in past years, I knew these unfair generalizations would be grossly insufficient to describe what I was about to experience in full.

The first day was a good warm-up exercise to what I would experience over the coming week. The terrain was easy, in Colorado terms, ten and a half miles of rolling foothills, stepping across small streams, shuffling through occasional sage fields, and dipping in and out of aspen groves dispersed among fragrant pine forests. Although it was the weekend, the COVID scare had kept the trail population lower than what I was expecting.

After crossing Cache Creek and the final 400-foot climb of the day I reached the top of the rise above Clear Creek with Mounts Oxford and Belford up to my right, Clear Creek Reservoir down to my left, and County Road 390 cutting through Clear Creek Canyon toward Vicksburg and Winfield. These two are now restored ghost towns that remain from the gold and silver rush of the late 1800s. One should take the opportunity to visit these sites, as they offer a true old Colorado experience. Rockdale and Beaver City were also two lesser known towns along this road that have much less to see.

Figure 200 The view up Clear Creek Canyon

It was from this view I met a father-daughter duo. The daughter was maybe 12 years old. It was her first backpacking trip. Her dad had hiked the Appalachian Trail when he was younger. He was excited to be the first to introduce her to life on the trail and by all accounts it seemed to be producing the expected result. She was quite content, taking a snack and a great view from the shade along the edge of the forest. Although they had just begun their trek a couple miles ago, she was already full of stories. It would be great one day to hear about where the trail took her.

The remainder of the day was hiking through sage fields down to the banks of Clear Creek, just outside a public camping area where I made my home for the night in my newly acquired hammock and tarp setup.

A couple hours after I arrived at camp two young ladies arrived and camped about 150 feet up river from me. Their goal was to hike the entire CT and were looking forward to getting their first 20-mile day the next day.

One of them came by while I was cooking dinner and asked if I could fix the solar charger panel they had been carrying. It apparently wasn't working. My meager attempt to explain why such a charger would be mostly ineffective while hiking through a forest, was of no help in their situation. They both had phones with nearly exhausted batteries and at least a couple days until they could find a place to charge again. I allowed them to charge from the ample 20,000 mAh battery bank I had brought with me. I also suggested they pick up a battery bank in the next town. Although we come out here in part to separate ourselves from the entrapment of our devices, these can be helpful navigation and emergency devices.

The older of the two ladies was a first-year college student who was coaxed into accompanying a teenage cousin on the trail this summer. Why not? It's the perfect thing to do at that stage in life. I must admit I was a little envious, not having such an opportunity when I was that age. And their spirits emanated the carefree lifestyle that tends to demonstrate so well through people in such a place in life, in such a place as the Colorado Trail.

Figure 201 Day 1 CT East Camp

The night was comfortable and calm. By 6:30 a.m. I was up and ready to hit the trail. Day two became the biggest day of the trip. I covered nearly 15 miles and 5000 feet in elevation gain, hiking from Clear Creek to Three Elks Creek.

I passed the first two of the Collegiates: Mounts Belford and

Oxford. One can catch a clear view of Oxford while stopping 6.5 miles up the trail at Pine Creek. This is where I met a man who was scouting out some fishing spots to later show his son. He had cowboy camped the night before under a towering ponderosa pine tree. I interrupted his time reading a novel, feet kicked up on a log, just soaking in the breezy day and fresh mountain air. We made small talk about gear and life on the trail as I took down a quick snack and filtered some water.

Figure 202 View of Mount Harvard, trail heading down to Pine Creek

At 1.5 more miles up the trail is the cutoff for Rainbow Lake, a popular day trip and backpacker destination for a relaxing weekend. I met several hikers heading that way.

Several more miles later, along a stretch with fantastic views of four Collegiate peaks to the west (Oxford, Belford, Harvard, and Columbia) and the Arkansas River Valley to the east, I took a short rest.

Figure 203 Collegiates to the West

The next landmark was Frenchman Creek, where I hike several years earlier on my way to summit Mount Columbia. I filtered more water here and hiked the remaining three miles to camp for the night above Three Elks Creek and a short distance from Harvard Lakes.

If one were to follow Three Elk Creek to its headwaters, it would be at the bottom of an astonishing cirque below Mount Columbia, surrounded on three sides by towering granite faces.

There are plenty of camping spots in the area around Harvard Lakes and Three Elk Creek. I arrived at camp around 5 p.m. and set up my hammock just as a storm moved through. Hanging in my hammock under my tarp to the therapeutic rhythm of the rain after a hard trail day was just what I needed. It broke long enough for me to fix my final meal of the day and settle in for the night. The stormy weather continued until about 1 a.m. I love sleeping in the rain.

Figure 204 Three Elks Trail and CT Intersection

Day three began with a nice stroll past Harvard Lakes as the sun was making its introduction to the day. A couple miles later, after crossing Powell Creek I stopped for breakfast with a nice view of the fading Buffalo Peaks across the Arkansas River Valley. I would round a 10,000-foot peak to catch a glimpse of Birthday Peak at the western end of North Cottonwood Creek Valley. Dark clouds were looming already to the west. I suspected I was heading into some weather.

At North Cottonwood Creek the trail began a 2600-foot ascent to the saddle on the east ridge of Mount Yale. It would follow Silver Creek for most of the way. This marked the passing of the 5th of the Collegiate Peaks.

Just before crossing Silver Creek, the trail opened up to an amazing view of Mount Yale. In the foreground was a marshy meadow and small pond. On the northern end was the ruins of an old mining cabin nestled along the edge of a pine forest. The scene couldn't be more perfect. It was the perfect place to rest and take in the view. As much as I wanted to stay here for the rest of my life, I needed to press on toward the saddle.

Figure 205 Mount Yale

At just over 11,600-feet, thunder started to rumble, the wind swirled and began threatening the demise of weakened pines from the beetle infestation, and then the hail started. I took out my umbrella to create a hand-held shelter from the storm in a small cluster of trees that had been spared the beetles. It was quite effective against the couple inches of hail that covered the forest floor within minutes. This made the trail slick for the final 400 feet of climbing. By the time I reached the saddle a short distance later, the storm had moved east, clearing the way for an unobstructed view of the more usual deep blue rocky mountain skies. The brilliant sun shone again, lapping up puddles now quickly disappearing along the trail.

Just under three miles in full descent, I arrived at Middle Cottonwood Creek, crossing County Road 306 just west of Rainbow Lake. In this area a year previous it had suffered the devastation of several avalanches. A massive pile of logs lay haphazardly in the valley, scattered like a monster size pile of pickup-sticks. I was awestruck by the ruins and the sheer power of nature. The mind plays a video of what the scene must have been like as this massive wall of snow, ice, and debris rumbled down these hills, its only foe was the thickening forest and the opposing rise of the other side of the valley. It's natures balance.

The trail continued, now parallel and eastward along Middle Cottonwood Creek until crossing County Road 344 and South Cottonwood Creek. It was near here I made my camp for the day before the trail began yet another ascent. This day of hiking realized 12.5-miles and 3200 ft elevation gain.

A young couple camped near me. We talked for a little while, as strangers on the trail often do. People who spend time in wild places don't waist any time making friends; we are friendly by default. There is an instant and spontaneous kinship. We take care of each other out here; we're bonded through our love of nature.

Figure 206 Mount Yale, now from the southeast along South Cottonwood Creek.

Day four was a low impact day with 13.5 miles and only 2000 ft elevation gain, past Mount Princeton and the Princeton Hot Springs Resort to my camp at Chalk Creek. This was another day of great views. The Arkansas River Valley was on my left and Mount Princeton on my right.

I decided to stop by Princeton Hot Springs Resort to see if I could take in a shower. By this time, some businesses were beginning to open with restrictions due to the COVID pandemic. There was a line out of the main lobby entrance. They were allowing only one person in at a time to address needs.

After watching the slow pace of the line I decided that exchanging an afternoon on the trail and a relaxing swing in my hammock next to a mountain creek with a long wait for a shower would be cheating myself of this great experience. So, I finished my snack, got back on my feet, and started walking toward a happier ending to this day.

Today was my exit from the foothills of the Collegiates, but not to the end of the trail. I had no rain today and the 5.5-mile road-walk from the Mount Princeton Road to camp was hot. Again, I'm glad I brought my umbrella to walk in the shade!

The road to my Chalk Creek camp for the night didn't have much traffic. It turned from paved to dirt shorty after leaving the resort. There was an occasional small farmhouse and several summer vacation homes nestled among pines and cottonwood trees with Chalk Creek gently swaying through the center of the valley. It was all very green and cool compared to the rest of the road walk. The sound of farm animals along the way reminded me of growing up in the Midwest, a peaceful, content existence. The north side of the valley rose quickly to form several hundred feet of sheer white cliffs. The color of this rock is caused by a high content of kaolinite, a soft mineral produced by hot springs percolating through cracks in the mountain over many imaginable years.

My hammock hung just a few feet from the creek that night. One good thing about sleeping in a hammock is that condensation does not form inside my tarp like it does in my tent when camping near creeks. It's just open space under my tarp with the therapeutic sound of the creek constantly reminding me that I'm not in a crowded place with human noise.

There were more people camped nearby and the summer day hikers didn't clear out until later in the day. But I still had a sense of isolation near the creek and enjoyed the end of my day just the same.

Figure 207 Camped along Chalk Creek

The fifth day brought me closer to the southern end of the Sawatch Range that hosts these great Collegiates and eight of the twenty highest peaks in the Rocky Mountains. The terrain was mixed with more pine forest runs, an occasional mountain meadow, smooth and easy rolling hills, some rocky parts as I've come to expect, and several great vistas including the merging north end of the Sangre de Cristo Mountains. I went through some open cattle ranges, crossed several streams, and earned some decent elevation gain.

The trail brought me through Lipe Meadow. This is named after John Lipe, a long-time Colorado Trail maintenance crew leader and Colorado Trail Foundation board member. I also passed a familiar trailhead to access trails that lead up to Mount Shavano and Tabeguache Peak, the Blanks Gulch Trailhead. I remember this trailhead from my peak-bagging days. It was here that I met a father waiting for his sons to come back down to the trailhead. Storms were brewing above treeline. He was a bit concerned for their safety, as these monsoonal patterns bring dangerous lightning.

Figure 208 Shavano - Tabeguache Trail intersection

About two miles later I finished my day at the North Fork South Arkansas River after 15.2 miles and 3600 feet elevation gain. It was near the Angel of Shavano Campsite where several campers were parked. I camped on the other side of the river far enough away to enjoy some solitude.

One thing I noticed today was that I have had little cell service this whole trip at my camp sites. Having no electronic pests is one of the pleasures of being out here.

With only 19 miles to go, the next two days could be somewhat leisurely, but not on the sixth day.

The last obstacle of this trip is the hike up Foose Creek which extends from the intersection of CO-50 to the end of the Colorado East segments.

Early on day six, after the first 5 miles, I crossed CO-50. Just above the highway one can see the end of the trail some 9 miles away near Peel Point just above the saddle where the trail intersects with the Collegiate West Route.

To know that the end of my Colorado Trail adventure was in sight is both exhilarating and filled me with a sense of gratitude. I was excited to finish but quieted by the complete blessing it was to have walked this entire trail. This chapter of my hiking experience would soon be over. My mind soon drifted into ideas about what I would do next. But I didn't get all caught up in that. I wanted to soak in these last steps, burn them in my mind. My pace began to slow; my eyes took in every sight; my ears absorbed every sound; I wanted to catalogue each moment in my memory with a promise never to forget this journey.

There is a three-mile road walk after crossing CO-50. It was along this road I met John. He had a great story. He was a retired corporate engineer turned hippie from Missouri. During the past several hot and humid Missouri summers he came up to Colorado to enjoy the cool mountain air and solitude by section hiking the Colorado Trail. He was now nearly halfway through. We talked until his turn around time when he had to return to his camp site and truck to move on to his next section.

I also met a young lady living the van life. She had parked her van (home) next to Foose Creek the night before. No kidding, she had a long flowing dress on with flowers in her hair, sandals, and eyes that were incredibly wide and full of wonder. She told a story of her spending time hiking in Europe and then on a long road trip throughout the southern part of the U.S., fully engaged in the free spirit lifestyle. I was back in the 60s, I swear.

It's these type of people we meet along on trail, those who are living life in full and taking in all the beauty around them, shedding their 9-to-5, soul-sucking, unfulfilling lives for something far less complicated – embracing the simple life - these are my people now.

All along Foose Creek it is incredibly lush. The undergrowth was as a garden in full bloom. Wildflowers surrounded me the entire way. All this muted the normal effect of thousands of dead trees left standing due to the pine beetle kill. I very much enjoyed the trail today.

Figure 209 Flowers along Foose Creek

This morning was clear, but as it was still in the season of monsoonal patterns, the afternoon turned cloudy and cooler as I began to climb the 3300 feet of elevation for the day.

I put in only 12 miles before setting up camp. It was difficult finding a place to hang among all the dead trees. But, even for tent camping, there were not many places to camp along this trail for most of the way. It's steep on both sides of the creek from before the last footbridge to the top, less than halfway up.

The final day was one word: incredible. I was up with the sun and on the trail early, eager to kiss the sign marking the end of my trail. The clouds moved out in the early morning. I passed several other hikers who had somehow camped in unlikely places along the way the night before. It seemed to get steeper as I approached the end.

Figure 210 The final steps ahead to the saddle

I summited the top of Foose Creek with a celebration! No more nagging. I finally completed the Colorado Trail!

Figure 211 The end of my Colorado Trail adventure

From the trail intersection on top of Foose Creek, where the east and west route meet, it's a 5-mile hike to the crest of Monarch Pass were Bobbi picked me up. This last five-mile stretch was surreal with a wild mix of emotions. I stopped several places along the way to soak in the views, talk with other hikers, and silently reflect on the 567 miles I had hiked, the people I met, and the incredible, irreplaceable memories.

I can easily say that the Colorado Trail has been one of the high lights of my life. It was not an easy thing to do. It was not always enjoyable. But it has brought me joy, a sense of accomplishment, and a renewed purpose. That purpose is to encourage others to get outside, enjoy God's awesome creation, dissolve into the pureness of nature, and to give ourselves permission to let go.

We all know too well that the world can be a harsh place. Among all the negative, pause once in a while and take the time to be good to yourself. That's the message. And when your day comes, I hope by then you will have finished completely the thing you were meant to do, the person you were purposed to be.

BIBLIOGRAPHY

Alvarez, Ted. 2017. "9 Bear Safety Tips From a Bear Biologist." *Backpacker.* September 28. https://www.back-packer.com/survival/the-truth-about-bears-the-skills.

2018. *Arnica.* https://www.webmd.com/vitamins/ai/ingredi-entmono-721/arnica.

Barker, Jason. 2003. "The Western Pine Beetle and Forest Health: Historical Approaches and Contemporary Conse-quences." *American Entomologist.* https://watermark.sil-verchair.com/ae49-0142.pdf?
token=AQECAHi208BE49Ooan9kkhW_Ercy7Dm3ZL_9C f3qfKAc485ysgAAAlAwggJMBgkqhkiG9w0BBwagg-gI9MIICOQIBADCCAjIGCSqGSIb3DQEHATAeBglghkgBZQ-MEAS4wEQQMgjfrgDGcK_omZYTyAgEQgIICA2osvg-f8uO6XRz0hp_Qbu1VenbQMWmR407nE5h6EtfXrr.

Brown, Lachlan. 2017. "15 Critical Secrets of Mentally Tough People." *Hack Spirit*, December 2. https://hackspir-it.com/15-traits-youre-mentally-tough/.

Bumgardner, Wendy. 2018. "The Healthy Way to Walk Down-hill." *VeryWell Fit*, October 7. https://www.verywell-fit.com/how-to-walk-downhill-3435572.

Bureau, United States Census. n.d. https://www.census.gov.

Canada, Government of. 2018. *Natural Resources Canada.* https://www.nrcan.gc.ca/forests/fire-insects-disturbances/top-insects/13381.

CDC. 2009. "A Guide to Drinking Water Treatment and Sanita-tion for Backcountry and Travel Use." *Centers for Disease Control and Prevention.* April 10. Accessed 2018. https://www.cdc.gov/healthywater/drinking/travel/backcoun-try_water_treatment.html.

Doran, Jeff. 2018. "Hiking Technique: The Rest Step." *Active.* https://www.active.com/outdoors/articles/hiking-technique-the-rest-step.

Elaine K. Luo, MD. 2017. "Rattlesnake Bite." *Healthline.* July 26. https://www.healthline.com/health/rattle-snake-bite#treatment.

2018. *Ethical Harvesting of the Arnica Flower.* http://www.arnica.com/about-arnica/industry-news/harvesting-wild-arnica-flower/.

Florida, University of. 2018. *Featured Creatures.* http://entnemdept.ufl.edu/creatures/trees/southern_pine_beetle.htm.

Heid, Matt. 2013. "Know This Hiking Book Lacing Technique: The Heel Lock." *Appalachian Mountain Club.* September 24. https://www.outdoors.org/articles/amc-outdoors/know-this-hiking-boot-lacing-technique-the-heel-lock.

Hood, Grace. 2014. "Soldierstone." *Kunc Hidden Colorado.* November 11. http://hiddencolorado.kunc.org/soldier-stone/.

Identities, WorldCat. 2018. *Bay Area Genealogical Society (Wis.).* http://worldcat.org/identities/nc-bay%20area%20genealogical%20society%20wis/.

2018. *Inter-Laken Hotel.* https://coloradoencyclopedia.org/article/inter-laken-hotel.

Lindsey, Joe. 2017. "What to do When You Get Caught in a Lightning Storm on Your Bike." *Bicycling.* October 31. https://www.bicycling.com/training/a20021271/getting-caught-in-storm-on-bike/.

Maloney, Lisa. 2017. *Moose Safety for Hikers.* April 5. https://www.thoughtco.com/moose-safety-for-hikers-1766332.

Mariama, Karima. 2015. "4 Characteristics of People Who Are Mentally Tough." December 24. https://www.success.com/4-characteristics-of-people-who-are-mentally-tough/.

Mitchell, Kirk. 2018. "Updated for 2018: 20 largest wildfires in Colorado history by acreage burned." *Denver Post.* July 4. https://www.denverpost.com/2018/07/04/20-largest-wildfires-in-colorado-history-in-acreage-burned/.

Rathbun, Kevin. 2016. "Why are some people mentally strong while others aren't as much? Is it mostly genetics?" *Quora*, October 30. https://www.quora.com/Why-are-some-people-mentally-strong-while-others-arent-as-much-Is-it-mostly-genetics.

Ruble, Eric. 2018. "San Juan National Forest to close Tuesday due to wildfire concerns." *Fox 31 News.* June 11. https://kdvr.com/2018/06/11/san-juan-national-forest-to-close-tuesday-due-to-wildfire-concerns/.

Schreiner, Casey. 2018. "Trail Etiquette: Who Has the Right of Way?" *REI.* https://www.rei.com/blog/hike/trail-etiquette-who-has-the-right-of-way.

Service, Colorado State Forest. 2018. *Mountain Pine Beetle.* https://csfs.colostate.edu/forest-management/common-forest-insects-diseases/mountain-pine-beetle/.

Service, National Park. 2018. *Isle Royale, Your Invitation to a Superior Wilderness.* https://www.nps.gov/isro/.

Simonovich, Ryan. 2018. "Previously Closed Trails and Roads Re-open Near Burn Areas." *The Durango Herald.* July 12. https://durangoherald.com/articles/231511.

Society, Wisconsin Historical. 2018. *Langlade, Charles Michel 1729-1801.* https://www.wisconsinhistory.org/Records/Article/CS1667.

Thomas, Liz. 2017. *Long Trails - Mastering the Art of the Thru-Hike.* Rowman & Littlefield.

Wildlife, Colorado Parks and. 2018. "Coyotes." *Colorado Parks and Wildlife.* http://cpw.state.co.us/learn/Pages/LivingwithWildlifeCoyote.aspx.

—. 2018. *Mountain Lions.* https://cpw.state.co.us/lions.